BARKING MAD

Two Centuries of Great Dog Stories

BARKING MAD

Two Centuries of Great Dog Stories

TOM QUINN

Quiller

Text © 2015 Tom Quinn
Illustrations © 2015 Nicola L Robinson

First published in the UK in 2015
by Quiller, an imprint of Quiller Publishing Ltd

British Library Cataloguing-in-Publication Data
A catalogue record for this book is available from the British Library

ISBN 978 1 84689 209 7

Illustrated by Nicola L Robinson

Design and typesetting by Paul Saunders

Printed in China

Quiller

An imprint of Quiller Publishing Ltd
Wykey House, Wykey, Shrewsbury, SY4 1JA
Tel: 01939 261616 Fax: 01939 261606
E-mail: info@quillerbooks.com
Website: www.quillerpublishing.com

You think dogs will not be in heaven?
I tell you, they will be there long
before any of us.

Robert Louis Stevenson

CONTENTS

Introduction 11

Chapter One • ECCENTRIC 15

Chapter Two • HEROES 43

Chapter Three • SPORTING 83

Chapter Four • SENTIMENTAL 103

Chapter Five • SUPER CLEVER 141

Chapter Six • MAD OWNERS 179

Bibliography 206

I am my master's dog at Kew,
Pray tell me, Sir, whose dog are you?

Lines written by Alexander Pope in 1738 for the collar
of Frederick Prince of Wales' favourite spaniel.

I had rather hear my dog bark at a crow,
than a man swear he loves me.

William Shakespeare, *Much Ado About Nothing*

I care not for a man's religion if his dog
and cat be not better for it.

Abraham Lincoln

Up with some little discontent with my wife upon her saying that she had got and used some puppy-dog water, being put upon it by a desire of my aunt Wight to get some for her, who hath a mind, unknown to her husband, to get some for her ugly face.

The *Diary* of Samuel Pepys, Tuesday, 8 March 1663

INTRODUCTION

THE BRITISH LOVE of dogs is legendary. Other nations cannot understand our obsession. Where much of the world dislikes, abuses or even eats its canines – the British, among other things, train them to help the blind, to herd sheep, to look for drugs and to rescue the victims of natural disasters.

The British have long understood that dogs also make marvellous companions and if treated well will reward their owners by guarding their houses, rescuing their children from ponds and fires and carrying their newspapers.

Our love for dogs is also reflected in the remarkable number of dog shows that fill the summer calendar – everything from countless small village shows to grand international events such as Crufts – and in the fact that for centuries the Royal family has led the way in its affection for spaniels, Labradors, and, perhaps most famously, corgis.

Countless books and articles have been written about the remarkable loyalty, intelligence and bravery of dogs and thousands of newspaper stories down the centuries record the antics, sometimes comic and sometimes tragic, of man's best friend.

For this book I have trawled through a vast number of these long forgotten books and newspapers to find what I hope are the most entertaining – and frequently astonishing – dog stories.

Here you will find tales of dogs rescuing their owners from flood and fire, dogs buying their own lunch, singing for their supper, travelling the country by train, firing cannons in the heat of battle and even helping to preach an occasional sermon.

Chapter One

ECCENTRIC

Monkey Business

A DOG NAMED Monkey, small, black and white of the cocker race, was reared by the groom of a gentleman in Ireland. Monkey was a general favourite, and roamed at his pleasure about the house and grounds.

One day his attention was attracted to the cook, who was busily engaged in pickling herrings; and, to her surprise, begged very impatiently for some. At length she threw him a damaged herring, intending thereby, as he was a dog of pampered appetite, to convince him that she had nothing suited to his tooth. He, however, snatched it eagerly, instantly disappeared, and returned in two minutes, asking earnestly for another.

The cook's curiosity was now excited, and, following the dog, she found that Monkey carried it, as he had the other, to Warden, a large bloodhound, who was constantly chained up, to whose less fastidious taste they both proved alike acceptable. Monkey followed the cook, and asked for a third herring; but his request was this time refused.

In the days that followed it was observed that Monkey delivered almost every scrap of food he came across to his enchained companion. When he himself was fed in his favourite bowl, Monkey was observed to eat with a sad countenance and having eaten only half his portion would grasp the edge of the bowl in his teeth and deliver it to his best friend. For life the two remained inseparable.

Charles Williams, Anecdotes of Dogs, 1870

Humorous Hound

Does the following dog story show a sense of humour?

A retriever was in the habit of leaving his bed in the kitchen when he heard his master descending the stairs in the morning. On one occasion a new kitchen-maid turned him out of his bed at a much earlier hour than usual. He looked angrily at her, but walked out quietly.

Time passed, and he was nowhere to be found. At last, in going to her bedroom, the kitchen-maid found him coiled up in her own bed.

B.B., The Spectator, 6 February 1875

Nelson's Hardy

I SHOULD LIKE to be allowed to help preserve the memory of a most worthy dog-friend of my youth, well remembered by many now living who knew Greenwich Hospital some thirty or five-and-thirty years ago.

At that time there lived there a dog pensioner called Hardy, a large brown Irish retriever. He was so named by Sir Thomas Hardy, when Governor (Nelson's Hardy), who at the same time constituted him a pensioner, at the rate of one penny per diem, for that he had one day saved a life from drowning just opposite the hospital.

Till that time he was a poor stranger and vagrant dog – friendless. But thenceforward he lived in the hospital, and spent his pension himself at the butcher's shop, as he did also many another coin given to him by numerous friends. Many is the halfpenny which, as a child, I gave Hardy, that I might see him buy his own meat – which he did with judgment, and a due regard to value.

When a penny was given to him, he would, on arriving at the shop, place it on the counter and rest his nose or paw upon it until he received two halfpennyworths, nor would any persuasion induce him to give up the coin for the usual smaller allowance.

I was a young child at the time, but I had a great veneration for Hardy, and remember him well, but lest my juvenile memory might have been in fault, I compared my recollections with those of my elders, who, as grown people, knew Hardy for many years, and confirm all the above facts. There, indeed, was the right dog in the right place. Peace to his shade!

J. D. C., *The Spectator*, 17 February 1877

Dance Troupe

VARIOUS AND wonderful in all ages have been the actions of dogs; and I should set myself to collect, from poets and historians, the many passages that make honourable mention of them. I should compose a work much too large and voluminous for the patience of any modern reader, but as the politicians of the age and men of gravity may be apt to censure me for misspending my time writing the adventures of a lapdog when there are too many modern heroes whose illustrious actions call for the pen of an historian; it will not be amiss to detain the reader in the entrance to this work with a short panegyric on the canine race to justify my undertaking it.

And can we without the basest ingratitude think ill of an animal that has ever honoured mankind with his company and friendship from the beginning of the world to the present moment?

While all other creatures are in a state of enmity with us, some flying into woods and wildernesses to escape our tyranny and others requiring to be restrained with bridles and fences in close confinement dogs alone enter into voluntary friendship with us and of their own accord make their residence among us.

Nor do they trouble us only with officious fidelity and useless goodwill, but take care to earn their livelihood by many a meritorious service; they guard our houses, supply our tables with provision, amuse our leisure hours and discover plots to the government. Nay I have heard of a dog making a syllogism which cannot fail to endear him to our two famous universities where his brother logicians are so honoured and distinguished for their skill in that useful science. After these extraordinary instances of sagacity and merit it may be thought ludicrous, perhaps, to mention the capacity they have often discovered for playing at cards, fiddling, dancing and other polite accomplishments, yet I cannot help relating a little story which formerly happened at the playhouse in Lincoln's Inn Fields.

There was at that time the same emulation between the two houses as there is at present between the great commonwealths of Drury Lane and Covent Garden, each of them striving to amuse the town with various feats of activity when they began to grow tired of sense, wit and action. At length the managers of the house at Lincoln's Inn Fields, possessed with a happy turn of thought introduced a dance of dogs who were dressed in French characters to make the representation more ridiculous and acquitted themselves for several evenings to the universal delight and improvement of the town.

But one unfortunate night a malicious wag behind the scenes threw down among the dogs the leg of a fowl which he had brought hither in his pocket for that purpose.

Instantly all was in confusion; the marquis threw off his peruke, mademoiselle dropped her hoop petticoat, the fiddler threw away his violin and all fell to scrambling for the prize that was thrown among them.

Francis Coventry, *The History of Pompey the Little*, 1751

Spade Work

A DOG I HAD IN 1851 and for three years afterwards was a handsome Newfoundland, and one of the most intelligent animals with which it was ever my good luck to meet. I was living in a village about three miles from Dover, where I did all my shopping and marketing, being generally my own 'carrier'.

Sometimes Nep would carry home a small parcel for me, and always most carefully. On one occasion Nep was with me when I chose a spade, and asked the ironmonger to send it by the village carrier. The spade was put by, labelled and duly addressed. I went on to have a bathe, my dog going with me, but on finishing my toilet in the machine, and calling and whistling for Nep, he was nowhere to be seen.

He was not to be found at the stable where I had left my horse, but on calling at the ironmonger's shop I found he had been there and had carried off the spade which I had bought, balancing it carefully in his mouth. When I reached home, there Nep was, lying near his kennel in the stable-yard looking very fagged, but wearing a countenance of the fullest self- satisfaction, and evidently wishing me to think he had fulfilled his dog-duty. My friend Mr Wood, who was a thorough lover and admirer of dogs, was delighted to hear of his intelligent performance.

Nep was also remarkable in other ways. Whenever I swam in the sea he would circle me howling quietly. Once he clearly thought I had got into trouble as I began coughing. He immediately began to nudge me hard towards the shore and would not stop until I had left the water.

Canophilist, *The Spectator*, 9 February 1895

Jukebox Hound

IF YOUR OWN smart dog is looking, perhaps you had better hide this book when you get through reading it. Don't leave it lying around where he can get hold of it. It might not be good for his morals. I hate to glorify mooching, but, try as I may, I can't get away from the feeling that the honour of being our lead-off mutt must go to Billy the Panhandler.

In defence of my decision, though, let me hasten to explain that it is not based entirely upon a perverse streak in my make-up. After all, Billy did lead an exemplary life of public service in his young manhood, and he richly deserved the recognition shown him.

It is regrettable, of course, that in his later years his weakness for weiners got the better of him and drove him to panhandling, but we must not let this lapse destroy our perspective of his life as a whole. After all, a few weaknesses in otherwise great characters only make them more human and draw us to them.

Billy was a crossbreed. His father was a bulldog, and his mother was an Airedale. He was owned by Finley Cartwright, an Osceola, Arkansas, hardware merchant, and everybody knew him. In fact, he was the town's official ratter. People borrowed Billy to help them kill the pests. In recognition for his public service, he was awarded a free dog license for life. The Cartwrights had other dogs that Billy didn't like, so he didn't spend much time at home. He divided his time between the Cartwright store and the home of some friends of his, Mr and Mrs C. L. Skatvold. They had an Airedale named Yank, and he and Billy were great pals.

The Skatvolds taught Billy to go to the store for packages of dog meat which were charged to their account.

He'd take them to Mrs Skatvold, and she'd open them and serve him and Yank. Billy wouldn't eat unless Yank got his share too. When Mr Skatvold, a safety expert with the U. S. Engineers was transferred to Memphis, they were heartbroken at having to say goodbye to Billy. Occasionally, though, Mr Skatvold had to return to Osceola on business, and whenever he met Billy on the street he would always take him to a hamburger stand or to a store and treat him. And that's what put panhandling ideas into Billy's head.

So Billy started bumming people on the street. He'd go up to a small group standing on a corner talking, and he'd look up at them and growl and whine. If that didn't produce results, he'd grab them by the pants legs and would otherwise annoy them till he got what he wanted – a nickel. A penny wouldn't do. He knew the difference. Then, with the nickel in his mouth, he'd trot off to his favourite grocery.

The man at the meat counter knew what Billy wanted when he saw him walk in – and well he should, for Billy was one of his steadiest customers – and he'd wrap up a couple of wieners. Billy would drop his nickel, take the package and trot on back to his benefactor. He'd put the package down and then look up, a hungry, eager expression on his face .

His friend would open the package, toss the wieners to Billy – and down the hatch they'd go. I don't know what understanding dog-lover first interpreted Billy's mooching antics – perhaps it was someone who had seen Mr Skatvold treat him – but it didn't take long for the knowledge to spread and mooching became easy for Billy. People gave him nickels to see him spend them. He lost his ambition. It wasn't necessary that he work for a living, and I fear the town ratter became soft and lazy in office.

Although Billy was smart, he wasn't smart enough to keep out of the street. An auto finally got him. I printed a piece about him in my newspaper column shortly before he was killed, and it was reprinted by the *American Kennel Gazette* and the *Reader's Digest*. His fame was nation-wide.

'Billy was a lovable dog,' says Mrs Skatvold. A picture of him is one of her treasured possessions – even if he did turn out to be a panhandler.

And speaking of moochers, another favourite of mine is Rex the Jukebox Hound. As a matter of fact, if the truth were known, we might find that Rex is the great-grand-son of Billy the Panhandler. He, too, is a mongrel; he was born at Bassett, Arkansas, only a few miles from Billy's home, and he has a keen brain and a number of traits reminiscent of Osceola's famous dog about town.

Rex is a medium-sized, black and tan, shaggy pooch. He is still just a pup – only a little over eight months old as I write this – but already he is the most valuable employee of the Southern Cafe, a little beer bistro, in Joiner, Arkansas.

'Why, that dog can mooch more nickels for the juke-box than a pretty girl can,' says Leon Chamberlain, operator of the place. If you want to see some fun – and lots of customers do – just pitch a nickel up and let it fall on the floor.

Rex may not be anywhere in sight, but the sound of that nickel will bring him dashing out from under a table or from behind the counter. He grabs the nickel and scoots for the jukebox. A couple of jumps puts him on top of it – they keep beer cases stacked beside it for his convenience – and he deposits his nickel, sits down and nervously looks around for Leon or Mrs N.V. Lee, an employee. One of them rushes over and puts the nickel in the slot for him.

As the jukebox lights up and the music starts, Rex sits on top of it and listens. Sometimes he sits up like a statue, sometimes he stretches out comfortably, and sometimes he cranes his neck around the curved top and peers dreamily down at the spot from which the music is coming.

His favourite tune is 'Sunny Side of Life'. Running to the jukebox with nickels is Rex's own idea. He had seen people put nickels in that box, and apparently he liked what happened when they did. So one day when a couple of customers were playing crackaloo, Rex darted out, grabbed a nickel and ran to the jukebox.

That nearly convulsed everybody. More nickels were pitched out. And he has been at it ever since, enthusiastically encouraged by his boss. Rex has become such a valuable dog that Leon won't permit him to run around with other dogs.

When they go anywhere, Leon usually has Rex on a leash. It's a queer sight in a little town like Joiner for a big, grown man to be seen with a pooch on a leash – considered a bit sissy – but tall, black haired Leon doesn't mind. That jukebox hound is important to his business.

Leon acquired Rex in an unusual way, and the incident proves that it pays to be kind to dogs. 'One Saturday night a man came in and asked me to lend him a screwdriver,' Leon explains. 'He and his wife were moving from Bassett to Memphis, and their car had broken down in front of my place. He needed the screwdriver to try to fix it. He worked on it, but couldn't get it running, so they left it and went on by bus. Said they'd come back the next day and get it.

'The next afternoon about four I heard a hollering in that broken-down car, and I looked in and saw eight pups. They were shut up in it, and had been there since the night before so I fed 'em. I figgered the fellow would show up later in the day.

'The next day, though, he still hadn't come, and I fed the pups again, but I brought two into the cafe. Well, sir, it was a week before that fellow came back to get his car, and I fed the pups all the time. And with six of 'em still in the car, you can imagine the mess they made.

'I learned the mother dog had jumped out of the car and got killed on the highway just before their car broke down that Saturday night. The fellow gave me the two pups I had brought into the cafe, and he took the other six on to Memphis. I named one of them Rusty and the other Rex. I gave Rusty to my brother out in the country, and I kept Rex. I don't know what kind of dog he is. He's just mixed.'

Maybe Rex will be the beginning of a new American breed: the jukebox hound.

Eldon Roarke, *Just a Mutt*, 1947

Bow Street Runner

Anyone who passes along Bow Street, Covent Garden, may observe that while one door of the police station is always open during business hours, for the magistrate, the officers, and the culprits, the other iron-gated doorway (No. 4) is but little used. There, in the year 1857, an old, starved, and sickly looking dog tried to make a home, but only to be driven away by the order of the superintendent again and again.

Subsisting on the charity of passers-by and of the men of the F division, whose headquarters are at Bow Street, the dog soon got hearty and strong, and having always returned to his chosen spot, now resisted all further attempts at removal.

As the various sections of police left the office to relieve the men on duty, the dog always followed them, and as soon as the last man's place was filled up invariably returned to the doorway. The men, in consequence, became so much interested in the dog that, on their encouragement, he took up his quarters inside the station, was named 'Charlie,' and even considered a member of the police force.

Received into the office, where, according to the police regulations, he had no right to be, Charlie, also known as the White Sergeant from his whiteness when clean, was placed on the mess; and at the Christmas dinner was allowed to sit at the table.

On state occasions, when the greater part of the division was required, a sergeant's armlet was buckled round his neck, and very proud he seemed to be of this decoration.

At the Victoria Cross presentation, in Hyde Park, all the divisions were represented by a large number of men, and 2,500 were on the ground. Charlie had been accidentally shut up in a room at the station; but as soon as he was set free, he went to the park, worked his way through the immense crowd that was collected, and took his station in front, at the head of his own division. The sergeant's armlet had been buckled round his neck, and as Charlie sat stiff and erect as an old soldier, in front of the long line of constables, Her Majesty, in passing, honoured the dog with a smile.

At a quarter to six every morning the first day relief is paraded in the station-yard, and then, and indeed at every parade, day and night, Charlie was present, marching up and down the front of the line with all the importance of a drill-sergeant.

On such occasions he was always accompanied by the only four-footed companion he was known to have – 'Jeanie,' the police-office cat, who, with a bell tinkling at her brass collar, trotted at his side.

Parade over, Charlie headed the relief in its march round the beats, when he generally set out on a tour of inspection round the district, waiting for a while with any policeman who might be a favourite. When, however, parade time drew near, no inducement could prolong his walk, but off he bounded, always reaching Bow Street in time to drill the section.

When the ten o'clock night relief went out, Charlie, after duly going the rounds, returned to sup with the men that had been relieved; but as soon as the meal was over he went out and took active duty, returning to the station in time for the quarter to two a.m. drill.

Only two exceptions occurred to his punctuality, and in each instance his absence was fully justifiable. Once Charlie watched for some days by the death-bed of an old constable to whom he was much attached; and on the other occasion he had been severely mauled and nearly poisoned by some of the thieves of the Seven Dials, to whom he was well known, and whose felonious schemes he had often assisted in defeating.

Many a tale is told of this kind; but one fact only can now be added. At an early hour one morning, a constable, while passing through New Church Court, a narrow lane off the Strand, was knocked down by two men. Charlie, who was a short distance behind, now ran across the Strand to the station in Somerset House, and seizing the sergeant on duty there by the greatcoat tail, led him to the constable's assistance, who was found to be severely wounded, and, apart from Charlie's sagacity, might have been killed outright. At length this interesting and useful creature became very feeble. No longer could he brave a rainy night. On getting wet he trotted to the station, and, after rolling himself about on the doormat, dried himself at the kitchen fire. If, when he had become thoroughly dry, the rain had passed off he again sallied forth; but if the rain continued, he sat with the constable on duty at the station door till the weather cleared up. Charlie died of old age, in front of the mess room fire in 1869.

Illustrated London News, July 1870

Learn from the Birds

I WAS STRUCK by many features in the character of a dog which I knew, illustrating, as I think, not only affection, but reasoning faculties, I shall acquaint you with a few of these, believing that they may be interesting, at least to all admirers of that noble animal.

When in India, I had a small rough terrier who, when given a bone, was sent to eat it on the gravel drive under an open porch in front of the bungalow. On several occasions two crows had made an attempt to snatch the dainty morsel, but their plans were easily defeated by Topsy's growls and snapping teeth. Away flew the crows to the branch of a tree nearby.

After a few moments of evident discussion, they proceeded to carry out a plan of attack. One crow flew down to the ground and gave a peck at the end of the dog's tail. Topsy at once turned to resent this attack in the rear, while the other crow flew down and bore the bone away in triumph.

The same dog had a favourite resting-place in an easy-chair, and was very often deprived of it by a dog which came as visitor to the house. Topsy did not approve of this, and her attempts to regain her seat were met with growls and bites.

This justified an act of eviction, and the busy little brain decided on a plan. The next day, as usual, the intruder established himself in the chair, which was close to the open door. Topsy looked on for a moment, and then flew savagely out of doors, barking at a supposed enemy. Out ran the other dog to see what was up, but when it came back Topsy had taken possession of the coveted seat. The other dog came slowly back, and curled himself up in a far-off corner.

The Spectator, 3 March 1888

Travelling Terrier

WHEN JOCK the Perth railway dog died, obituaries appeared in newspapers and he was mourned on both sides of the English Channel.

No one knew when Jock first appeared on the foot-plate – it was generally agreed to be about 1890 when he was still a puppy. From the first he was attracted to the engine rather than the carriages, but as the years went by and his tastes matured he did sometimes ride in more comfort than the driver and fireman could provide. He was much loved by all the railway staff simply because he was so friendly. He would sit quietly by the driver and somehow never manage to impede his work or that of the numerous firemen who knew and loved him.

Jock regarded the Scottish Central as his own particular railway, and Perth as his principal place of residence, but he made frequent trips to Aberdeen, Edinburgh, York and London. When he arrived at Perth station in the mornings – and he arrived ready to travel three or four times a week – the staff simply patted him and let him through without a ticket. He would then choose whichever train took his fancy, climb aboard and wait for the off.

Five years later he was a celebrity and drivers and firemen would be stricken at the sight of Jock climbing aboard someone else's train. On several occasions he got as far as Paris where a Perth businessman recognised his familiar face. Three days later the businessman was in Lyon and there, resting on the main platform, was Jock.

Wherever he went Jock always returned within a week or ten days to Perth and he was generally happy travelling with other commuters to Glasgow or Edinburgh.

Once he travelled to London and vanished for nearly three weeks. Among the drivers and firemen there was talk of nothing else. Then a railway official spotted Jock in a rough looking pet shop near King's Cross. The official protested to the shop owner who insisted he had come by Jock legitimately. There was nothing for it – the railway official handed over three pounds and Jock was released. Back at the station as soon as he was let down on the platform Jock ran about in an ecstasy of tail wagging and happy yelping. When the Edinburgh express arrived he was greeted tearfully by the crew before leaping aboard for the first part of his journey home.

When Jock died after more than ten years' happy travelling the Central Scottish Railway went into mourning. By the end it was estimated that his regular appearances around the station and his friendliness to everyone had made the Central Scotland a more prosperous railway company than it would have been without him. It was even said that people booked their tickets partly to get where they wanted to go and partly to meet up with their old friend Jock once again. No one claimed the little body when it was found that he'd died quietly in his sleep and his passion for railways was never explained but there is no doubt that railways were the love of his life.

Railway Times, 1912

Dining with the Earl

THE ECCENTRIC Earl of Bridgewater (1756–1823) never married. He rarely left his estate and as he grew older became ever more slovenly and bizarre in his habits. He made a servant follow him constantly carrying a large box of snuff; he insisted on wearing a different pair of shoes for every day of the year and he never threw anything away.

As a result his large London house groaned under the weight of old boxes and trunks, umbrellas, chests filled with old curtains, suits and rugs, discarded wrapping papers, broken down chairs and tables, innumerable pictures, books, papers and piles of assorted domestic refuse.

But among all his eccentricities there was one that distinguished Bridgewater from every other eccentric aristocrat in the land: his love for his dogs. He owned fifteen and he treated them as if they were his children. Some were strays he'd taken a fancy to while walking the streets; others were pure-bred hounds and gundogs, still others were tiny lapdogs. All were allowed to sleep with the Earl and to eat with him.

Indeed every day he would have his huge dining room table laid with the best linen and silver cutlery and each of the dogs would sit in a chair in its allotted place. The dogs were expected to dress for dinner and the only time the Earl shouted was if they jumped down before the meal was ended.

Several times a year the Earl travelled by train from London to his home in the country. Normally one or two dogs would accompany him, but on one extraordinary occasion all fifteen dogs came along. Bridgewater paid for fifteen first class tickets for the dogs and took over two whole compartments. To make sure no stranger tried to enter either of the two compartments – this was in the days when compartments could not be reserved – he sent his servants on ahead to the station to bar the entrances to the carriages in advance of the Earl and his party of dogs arriving at the station.

During the journey each dog took a seat in one or other of the compartments and the Earl wandered between the two making sure his favourites were enjoying themselves. Other passengers looking for a vacant seat found the blinds of the compartments drawn and the Earl's No Entry signs posted on the windows.

On one never to be forgotten journey Bridgewater fell asleep and on waking went to check on the dogs. He found to his horror that six entirely new dogs – 'I'd never met them before,' he declared later – had somehow joined his favourites. Unused to strange dogs the Earl's normally well behaved hounds were barking and jumping and biting each other.

It took the Earl and his servants some time to restore order and to reject the interlopers. Bridgewater was so outraged by what he described as a 'serious violation of his dignity' that he threatened the railway company with legal action and it was only a visit from one of the directors that smoothed the troubled waters. Though the railway company officials privately agreed the Earl was a damned nuisance he was a good customer with powerful friends – so the doggy train journeys continued and, so far as history records, without further mishap.

Eccentric Lives, 1955

Egg Surprise

ANYONE WHO has watched gundogs in action at a field trial will have been astonished at their intelligence, so it is perhaps not surprising that many gundog owners have taught their animals to do remarkable things, but few dogs can have mastered the trick a Victorian sportsman taught his Labrador.

He was a keen shooting man who regularly shot duck on the lakes and ponds on his farm. One lake had a small island in the middle on which the ducks often laid their eggs. Now this shooting man enjoyed eating duck eggs but didn't have a boat on the lake and so had no easy way to reach the nests.

Then he had an idea. He decided he would try to train one of his gundogs to swim across to the lake and retrieve the eggs without breaking them. Months later after numerous disasters the dog finally realised what was wanted. It had long ago got the hang of retrieving the eggs. The problem was to get the dog to bring the eggs back in one piece without eating them!

A juicy piece of beef used as a reward for success eventually persuaded the dog that it was better to delicately retrieve the egg rather than crush and eat it and from that day on the dog was frequently sent across to the lake whenever his master needed an egg for breakfast. In fact with repeated retrieves the dog would bring a whole nest-full of eggs back one at a time and without a single breakage.

But perhaps the most bizarre part of the tale is that a year or so after the dog began its occasional egg forays its owner happened to be at the lake very early one morning and he noticed an animal swimming. It was a fox. It is rare to see a fox swimming – unless it's in the process of escaping the hunt – so the man kept as well hidden as possible to see why the animal had taken to the water.

The fox reached the island in the middle of the lake and a few moments later could be seen swimming back with an egg in its mouth. It reached the shore and trotted off into the undergrowth with the egg held delicately in its jaws. Moments later it was back in the water and heading for the island. It made the journey back and forth four times. Each time it took the unbroken egg into the wood – clearly it was returning to its earth to feed its young.

On the fifth journey the fox reached the bank on its return journey and then very deliberately crushed the egg and swallowed it. Clearly the cubs had been fed, the nest was now empty and the fox needed its own breakfast!

The intriguing question was: had the fox been watching the Labrador swim to the island and simply copied it?

The Sportsman, March 1910

Dogs' Dinner

THE ENGLISHMAN's love for his dogs is legendary, which may explain why the Victorian Earl of Pevensey had himself buried with his favourite spaniel and Lord Derby dined every day with his ten dogs seated round the table, each in turn served by a team of flunkeys.

The crafty German scientist and entrepreneur Johannes Rohr decided to cash in on this passion for all things canine by designing what he described in his first printed advertisement as an Improved Humane Kennel for Man's Best Friend.

The basic idea of the kennel – which was to be produced in a range of designs from miniature Gothic castle to suburban villa – was that, using a Heath Robinson arrangement of weights and counterweights, it would keep the dog warm and cosy at all times.

How on earth did it work? Well, as the dog entered the kennel, its weight, as it stepped on a platform, operated a pulley that, in turn, released a catch that lowered a miniature duvet over the lucky animal. When the dog walked out of its kennel the system went into reverse mode and the duvet was lifted back up to the top of the kennel.

At first the difficulty was that dogs tended to bolt in terror as the cover was let down or they tried to eat the duvet; one poor animal managed to get tangled up in the pulley system. Hardly had the Improved Humane Kennel begun to take the pet world by storm when it was suddenly – and permanently – discontinued.

Robin Ward, *Mad Science*, 1950

Well Trained!

THERE ARE many stories concerning dogs travelling alone by train. Several dogs are known to have crossed the northern wastes of Russia on the trans-Siberian railway unaccompanied, and nearer to home dogs have accidentally hopped on to trains that have taken them hundreds of miles from their homes. At Reading at the end of the nineteenth century there was even a platform dog that ran around the station with a special leather collection box tied to its back collecting money for charity. It took regular trips to London, presumably hoping to raise even more cash for good causes. It was so popular that when it died it was stuffed and put in a big glass case on the platform and it was still there well into the 1970s.

But perhaps the most extraordinary animal traveller of all was a dog that with an instinct almost human always seemed to know where he wanted to go and how to get there. He was known as Railway Jack, and he belonged to a former stationmaster at Lewes who, in the early 1880s, was a frequent traveller on the trains between that station and London.

His railway knowledge was vast. He appeared to know all the trains up and down and travelled, so far as anyone could make out, for the pure love of it. He would often get out of the train at intermediate stations for a saunter in the countryside or to greet the rustic railway staff, but never missed the last train home.

A remarkable fact about Jack was that he was never known to take the wrong train. Once, when placed by a porter in the guard's van of a train that was not going to his destination, he appeared to sense in some extraordinary way that matters were not right – he jumped out and returned to the platform waiting room until his train to Lewes arrived.

He travelled all over the South East for years visiting all the major towns and many tiny villages where there were stations. Passengers were always delighted to see him; he was adored by schoolchildren and universally missed when at last he died.

Land and Water, September 1895

Chapter Two

HEROES

Sound Bites

THERE ARE many stories of dogs rescuing their owners –
or their owners' children – from flood and fire but a very
rare case occurred recently in Ireland.

A visitor to a remote village in the far west of that country had taken with him his old black retriever on a long
walk around a deep lough. It was a windy autumn day,
blustery in the extreme and white horses whipped across
the surface of the lough which was known to be twenty
feet deep and more just a few feet out from the bank.

The dog limped slowly along behind its master. It was
nearly twelve years old and in poor health but it was a
much loved pet and its owner, a Mr Kehoe, dreaded the
time when it would no longer be able to accompany him
on its daily walk.

The dog was a good swimmer but rarely entered the water now, content instead to amble along and then sleep the day away.

As the two reached a steep part of the bank they saw ahead of them a woman and a child. They exchanged good morning and carried on. Hardly had they passed the woman when there was a loud splash and on looking round Mr Kehoe saw that the young boy had toppled into the lough where the bank was steepest and therefore the water likely to be very deep indeed.

The mother had hardly had time to shout when the old retriever bounded back along the bank and plunged into the water. He quickly found the boy and caught his collar firm in his jaws. As soon as this was done the dog began quietly to swim in a narrow circle holding tight to the boy but keeping his head above water all the while.

Mr Kehoe quickly found a long branch and shouting to the boy persuaded him to grasp the stick firmly in both hands. It was then the work of a moment to bring the boy safely to the bank where his grateful mother quickly hauled him up the slope.

But the bank was too steep for the rheumatic legs of the canine rescuer. Mr Kehoe walked along the bank encouraging his dog all the while to follow him, at last they reached a place where the slope of the bank was more gentle and the dog was able to climb out of the freezing lough. As soon as he was on land he wagged his tail a little and then quietly fell in behind his master and resumed their walk.

What was perhaps most remarkable about the tale was not that an elderly dog had rescued a child but that the dog was completely blind.

Arthur Waugh, *The London Gazette*, 1888

Gunner Greyhound

MUSTAPHA, A STRONG and active greyhound belonging to a captain of artillery, raised from its birth in the midst of camps, always accompanied his master, and exhibited no alarm even in a battle.

In the hottest engagements it remained near the cannon, and carried the match to light the cannon in its mouth. At the memorable battle of Fontenoy, Mustapha's master, the captain of artillery, received a mortal wound. About to fire on the enemy, he and several of his corps were at that instant struck down to the earth by a furious firing, when the dog, seeing his master bleeding on the ground, became desperate, and howled piteously.

Nor did he merely give way to unavailing grief, for a body of French soldiers were now advancing to gain possession of the piece of ordnance, which was aimed at them from the top of a rising ground; when Mustapha, as if he would revenge his master's death, seized the lighted match with his paws and fired the cannon, loaded with case-shot.

Seventy men fell on the spot, and the remainder took to flight. After this bold and extraordinary stroke, the dog lay down sadly near the dead body of his beloved master, tenderly licked his wounds, remained with the corpse without any sustenance for twenty-two hours, and was even removed with great difficulty by some of the comrades of the deceased.

This gallant greyhound was taken to London, and presented to the king, George II, who ordered it to be taken care of as a brave and faithful public servant.

L'Histoire des Chiens Celebres, 1818

Burglar Bashing

A RARER TYPE OF canine hero is the dog who saves life by putting to rout bandits and assassins – dogs like Mickey Greer. Mickey, a rough-coated, medium-sized dog with Irish terrier blood in his veins, belonged to William Greer, a Philadelphia feed dealer.

Mickey was very fond of a neighbour, Mrs Margaret B. Mayer, and spent a lot of time at the garage she operated.

And that's where he was, asleep on a wicker sofa in the office, when at about nine-twenty a young man entered and asked for four cans of oil.

As Mrs Mayer turned to get them, he struck her over the head with an iron bar, and continued to beat her after she fell to the floor.

'As Mickey visited the garage enough to be accustomed to men using hammers, beating tyres and other objects, so he should be excused for not grasping the situation at once,' Charles E. Pyle, agent for the Pennsylvania Society for the Prevention of Cruelty to Animals said in his report to the American Humane Association.

'But when Mrs Mayer finally gave a weak cry, he went into action as only a brave dog would. Regardless of a blow on the head that gave him a scar for life, Mickey attacked the intruder with such ferocity that the man became frightened and fled. Mickey then turned his attention to Mrs Mayer, licking her face, pulling at her sleeve and whining. It was only this that kept her sufficiently conscious to crawl to the sidewalk where she was discovered by passers-by and rushed to a hospital. The doctor said that a few more minutes would have been fatal due to the loss of blood.'

After that the sofa in the office became Mickey's very own. He was welcome to sleep away his days on it, and he did – a look of contentment on his face.

Eldon Roarke, *Just a Mutt*, 1947

Chilkoot Saves a Stranger

CHILKOOT WAS so quiet and well-behaved that sometimes he was brought up from the kennels to make a call
at the house. It seemed to please him very much, and
Missy used to say: 'I'm sorry you can't come in every
day, Chilkoot. You certainly behave like a gentleman, but
you know that, after all, you are a sled dog, and sled dogs
ought to live out of doors.

'Your coat is too thick for you to be comfortable in our
warm house, and besides, all the other dogs would feel
hurt because they were not invited. You wouldn't want
to make them unhappy?'

Chilkoot seemed to understand. When the time
came for him to go back to the corral, he would run off
quite cheerfully, without teasing to stay longer. In fact,
he always tried to make the best of things. When Missy
and her guests came to visit the kennels he never seemed
to expect any special attention from them, even though
they had been so friendly at the house. He had a funny
little bark of greeting for them which seemed to say: 'Just
speak to me once and give me a pat as you go by. Then I
shall know that you haven't forgotten me.'

And no one who looked into his serious, honest eyes
could ever refuse him. Although Chilkoot was not an
especially large dog, he always made Missy think of the
big, faithful St. Bernards that are trained to rescue lost

travellers in the Swiss mountains. These dogs are saddled with packs which hold blankets and food and drink for those in need.

'When we are going for a climb,' Missy said one day, 'how useful it would be if our dogs could help us carry the wraps and the luncheon! We could easily train Nook and Chilkoot, and I think that they would like to do it.' Missy was right. Dogs that are well trained take pride in doing helpful things. Nook and Chilkoot soon learned to make themselves useful on these mountain picnics. The rule was that one dog should run ahead, never out of sight, to the end of the path, and that the other dog should carry the pack and follow the last member of the party.

In mountain climbing there are always some who have to go slowly, and who need help to reach the top. One day a party of eleven left the Farm to climb a famous mountain in the neighbourhood. For a while all went well. The dogs took turns in carrying the pack, and they were both skilful in following the trail through the woods and in finding the best path among the rocks.

Everybody agreed that never had mountain climbing been made so pleasant and easy. The day was perfect; there was no wind; and the air was clear. When, at length, the woods came to an end, the dogs again changed places, and Nook went ahead over the rocks. The trail grew steeper and steeper, and presently a few of the party suggested that it might be well to divide their number into two parts. This would allow the rapid climbers to push on to the top of the mountain, while the others could take as much time as they liked. This seemed to them all a good plan, and Nook led the first division upward with much waving of tail and an occasional bark of encouragement to his followers.

The final scramble brought them to the top, somewhat breathless, it is true, but in good condition, and they sat down to wait for the rest of the party. They had waited for some time when they noticed that Nook was restless and uneasy. He wandered back and forth, looking down the trail, and showing every sign of anxiety. He was plainly worried about Chilkoot. Missy called, the men whistled, but there was no answer. By this time the rest of the party had appeared, but they could not tell what had become of Chilkoot. Nook was trembling as if he were half frozen. He ran from ledge to ledge, followed by Missy, who was as troubled as he was. Where in the world was Chilkoot? There was no mistaking the appeal in Nook's eyes. 'Yes, go look for him,' said Missy, and away the dog bounded down the rough path. 'It's possible that some strange animal is giving Chilkoot trouble,' one of the men said.

'We'll take a rope and look him up. Maybe he has been pushed off one of these ledges and can't make his way up again.' So Missy and two of the men set off to follow Nook's flying feet. Long before they reached the spot where he had disappeared a distant bark answered their calls. It seemed to come from a deep ravine, lined with sharp rocks, which stretched far down the mountain side. Presently Missy called again, and this time she was answered by two barks.

'The dogs certainly are not running,' she said. 'The sounds come from exactly the same place. But how in the world can we get down there? It would be like climbing down the side of a house.'

Just then there was the noise of scrambling feet behind them, and Nook flung himself upon his mistress. But immediately he turned, as if to say, 'Follow me,' and was off along the edge of the cliff. After a run of a hundred feet or more he began to pick his way, slowly and carefully, down an almost invisible path.

Using the rope to tie themselves together so that they should not slip on the steep rocks, the three rescuers made their way to the foot of the ravine. There they found Chilkoot, sitting beside the motionless body of a strange man. Nook took his stand just beyond him, looking as wise and dignified as a human doctor might who has just brought his patient through a dangerous sickness. Chilkoot barked once in greeting, but made no other sign that he thought his work was ended.

'No, the man isn't dead,' said Missy, as she knelt beside the still form. 'He is stunned by the fall, but he is breathing. First aid is all that he needs, I think, unless he has broken some bones. Presently he can tell us what happened?'

'I was coming down this trail alone,' the stranger explained later, 'I suppose I must have slipped, for the first thing I knew I was lying on my back down here, and the top of the cliff, where I had been walking, seemed miles away. There was a sudden, sharp pain in my head, and I knew nothing more until I felt a warm tongue on my face. When I opened my eyes a great dog was lapping my face and hands and wagging his tail.

'I was so dazed for a few minutes that I really thought he might be a wolf until I saw the bundle on his back. I hope it was all right for me to help myself. That canteen of water was certainly the most refreshing drink I ever had. Then I tried to climb up the rocks, but I was so dizzy that I fell back again in a faint.

'Just before everything turned black I saw this other big yellow dog coming as hard as he could run along the edge of the cliff, and in another minute he was plunging through the bushes above my head. The two dogs put their noses together, and one rushed off to you while the other settled down beside me. How either of them got down here, or how they knew enough to send back for you, I don't know, but between them they seem to have saved my life. I hope I shan't prove ungrateful?'

Missy, who had an arm around the neck of each dog, gave them both a hug. She was not at all surprised to hear what they had done.

E. O. Seeley and M. A. L. Lane, *Chinook and His Family*, 1930

Spot the Dog

Spot, a fox terrier belonging to Mr and Mrs Richard Harmon of Brooklyn, won his bravery medal for quick thinking in a most unusual accident.

About one-thirty one morning Mr Harmon was startled out of a deep sleep when Spot began pulling at the bedclothes and barking frantically. He jumped up, switched on the light and saw a shocking sight that greatly increased his alarm. The pup's mouth was bloody!

Then Mr Harmon glanced at the bed. His wife wasn't in it! Spot turned and ran toward the cellar door, and the frightened master, his heart pounding, followed. At the bottom of the stairs, crumpled up in a little pool of blood, was the unconscious form of Mrs Harmon.

She was bleeding from a deep gash in her head. An ambulance was called, and she was rushed to a hospital. It was found that she had a compound fracture of the head, a broken collarbone, and was almost dead from the loss of blood.

She evidently had fallen down the stairs while walking in her sleep.

'The doctors gave Spot the credit for saving her life. They said he helped to stop the bleeding by licking the cut,' Mr Harmon said, 'and he gave the alarm just in time. She would have died if left very long without help.'

Eldon Roarke, *Just a Mutt*, 1947

Water Dog with a Difference

ANYONE WHO has the interests of dog breeding at heart is proud to be the owner of a well-bred specimen of the particular breed to which he devotes his attention.

But if the dog also happens to have earned the right to wear the *Daily Mirror* Brave Dogs' Collar, then indeed has his owner cause to be proud. Such is the happy lot of Mr Harry Harmer who lives at Wigan.

He is the owner of a thoroughbred bull terrier, Peggy, who has been awarded the coveted collar for saving a twelve-year-old boy from drowning. Peggy, like most of her breed, is a big, powerfully-built dog, and has a handsome white coat.

With a confidence born of her splendid physique, she fears neither man nor beast, yet is never happier than when playing with young children, or with Fanny, a black cat who shares with her the comforts of Mr Harmer's home.

She boasts an excellent pedigree; several champions are numbered amongst her forbears, and one of them was sold to an American breeder for over £200.

She was born in December, 1928. Her mother was a line bitch named Naria's Pal.

She performed the brave deed which won her distinction on 22 September 1929. It was a Sunday and she was out for a walk along the towpath of the Leeds and

Liverpool Canal. A young boy, Thomas Brown, was climbing the bank to reach some blackberries, when he missed his footing, slithered down the bank and fell into the canal. He was unable to swim and soon got into difficulties in the deep water.

He had gone under once and struggled to the surface, when Peggy sizing up the situation at a glance, leapt into the water and swam over to him. She caught hold of his clothes and managed to keep him up until other help was forthcoming.

Several people hurried to the rescue and dragged the boy to safety. As he was unable to swim, he would undoubtedly have been drowned but for Peggy's prompt action.

Every year Peggy attends the Wigan Carnival and collects for charity. She is an expert beggar and invariably manages to collect a considerable sum for the funds. Quite recently she gave a further display of her keen intelligence. Mr Harmer was awakened in the night by her furious barks, and on going downstairs found some clothes which had been left in front of the kitchen fire had been set alight by a live cinder. Without Peggy's barking the house might well have been burned to the ground and everyone in it.

Land and Water, August 1925

Chesapeake to the Rescue

CHESAPEAKE IN the fall of the year, 1926. From the Duchy of Waterbury, Connecticut, there came to Jansen one Dr Demming, equipped with all the necessary paraphernalia for getting his limit of ducks and geese.

The one thing he lacked was a good retriever, without which no self-respecting sportsman goes afield. George D. Lidster, a guide, to whom I might properly refer as the consort of Queen, came to the rescue.

'The old girl,' said he, 'is the equal of any water dog in the Dominion, but you must first be friends; win her confidence and make it plain that you appreciate the value of a good dog.'

Dr Demming, with that professional air common to medical men, established a relationship that eventually won the esteem of the Chesapeake. Her capitulation was complete and in a sense Providential. In the grey of the next morning, the east banked with heavy clouds and a wind blowing from the north – perfect conditions for Saskatchewan gunning.

George Lidster with one dog and Dr Demming with Queen swarmed into a prairie-fed auto and headed for Jansen Lake, which is crossed via the upper and the lower Jansen bridges, a mile apart.

Over these two wooden viaducts the birds from daybreak to ten in the morning pass in continual flight, the fanfare of guns recording the progress of sustained attack.

Lidster was joined by a third gunner at the upper bridge. The air was alive with flying birds. Echoes from the Doctor's stand on the lower bridge indicated that he was making the most of his opportunity. Presently the firing from that quarter ceased.

'I guess,' said Lidster, 'that the Doctor has got his limit and has quit shooting. Must have had good luck and picked 'em off fast. He can hit 'em all right.'

A few moments later the bark of a dog, breaking through the noise of the guns, attracted his attention.

'Hello, Queen. What's the matter, girl? Have you quit the Doctor?'

The Chesapeake, panting heavily, her tongue hanging out, trotted up to Lidster and began to whine. She then turned and took a few steps over the path by which she had come from the lower to the upper bridge.

Lidster spoke to her again. She came back whining, pulled at his sleeve and again started away, a queer expression in her eyes.

'Something has happened to Demming,' said Queen's master. 'That's what she is trying to tell me. Let's go.'

Following Queen, who had selected the shortest possible route to the lower bridge a mile away, the trio found Dr Demming sprawled on the planking in a welter of his own blood gushing with every heartbeat from a deep wound in the left wrist, a wound that exposed the arteries. He was unconscious.

To one side lay his shotgun, which had exploded at the breech. A fragment of the metal had entered his arm and passed eight inches upward. Nearby was a pile of green-headed mallard, canvas-backs, blacks and teal that Queen had retrieved earlier in the morning, a bag in which, following the tragedy to her new-made friend, she had lost all interest.

What concerned her now was the pale and insensible man on whose mangled arm George Lidster was twisting a tourniquet. During this operation the guide, without lessening his attention to the details of first aid, heaped expressions of endearment upon the dumb beast who had retrieved that precious thing called life, retrieved it for a comparative stranger whose friendly hand had become suddenly inert.

After three-quarters of an hour Dr Demming, recovering consciousness, was allowed to bestow a feeble caress upon the shaggy head of the Chesapeake, who seemed to know that her trip across the marsh had not been in vain.

In the speech of dogs she whined a tremulous farewell as the wounded man, hurried thirty-nine miles across country by automobile, caught the Canadian Pacific flyer, and was taken to a hospital in Saskatoon, where the fragment of gun metal was removed from his arm.

He recovered after three weeks of medical attention.

Six incomparable mornings on the lower bridge are stored
among my recollections, but the crown jewel in the Jansen
Duck Durbar is the Chesapeake retriever – Queen.

Robert Davies, *The More I Admire Dogs*, 1936

Doggy VC

Gyp earned the VC Collar for Brave Dogs when he was
only five months old. He was acquired by his master, Mr
Edwin Drew, of Streatham, from a stall in Brixton Market
Place.

Mr Drew wanted a dog as companion and house guard,
and remembered seeing a stall in the market on which,
from time to time, puppies were displayed for sale. On visiting this stall, he discovered three little puppies on view,
presumably all of the same litter, and finally selected Gyp
as being the best marked and sharpest of the three. It would
be hard to say what breed the dog's parents were, never-
the less Gyp has grown into a very handsome little dog. He
has a silky brown coat, set off by a dark streak down the
centre of the back, and white front paws and chest, whilst
his eyes are of a beautiful, soft, deep brown colour.

As a puppy, Gyp was tiny, and Mr Drew was able to
carry him home in his jacket pocket. He has, of course,
grown a certain amount since, but even now he is remark-
ably small for a terrier. Once when out for a walk in the

country, the little dog slipped down a rabbit hole and was only extricated with the greatest difficulty. Mr Drew bought Gyp in March, 1929, and in the summer of that year took the dog away with him when he went on his holiday; the decision to take Gyp was a most fortunate one, as will be seen later.

Mr Drew has three children, two boys and a girl, Charlie, Ronnie and Jennie, then aged twelve, ten and seven respectively, and the entire family spent the holiday motoring and camping in Wales. During the course of the tour, they went through Breconshire, and, finding the country surrounding a small village to their liking, they camped in a field adjoining a farm owned by a Mr Evans.

All went well for a day or two, and the children enjoyed themselves immensely roaming through the fields and farmyards in company with little Gyp, who, having a strong taste for excitement and adventure, must have considered himself in the seventh heaven of delight at being thus provided with such wide scope for exploration and all day in which to roam at will. Then, one evening, Mr Drew and his wife decided to drive into a neighbouring town after the children had been put to bed.

Before leaving, they saw that the family were safely asleep, and left a candle lamp of a safety pattern alight and suspended on the tent pole in case any of the children should awaken during their absence and feel at all nervous.

Shortly after they left though, a wind sprang up, and it seems that the lamp swung against the canvas and set it alight. The flames spread quickly down the side of the tent towards the flap entrance. The children slept on, blissfully unaware of the blaze over their heads.

But Gyp saw the flames, and young though he was, he appreciated the danger that threatened his companions. He had been left by Mr and Mrs Drew trotting about outside the tent, absorbed in some business or other of his own.

Gathering his small body up taut, he took one leap straight through the flames, then, bounding over to Ronnie, he scratched and pawed urgently at the sleeping boy's face. When one remembers the acute dread of fire inherent in practically all animals, it will be conceded that this was an exceptionally brave action for a puppy only five months old.

In response to the dog's frantic pawing on his face, Ronnie awoke and saw the danger. He quickly wakened his brother and sister, and the three just managed to crawl out under the rear of the tent before the whole structure collapsed in flaming ruin.

How narrowly the children escaped serious injury, perhaps even death, was shown by the fact that the flames had, as it was, badly singed Jennie's hair. Gyp, too, was burned all down his back.

Mr Evans, the farmer, was greatly impressed by Gyp's

gallant behaviour, and he it was who suggested that the dog's action deserved recognition. When Mr Drew returned home after the holidays, he got in touch with the Royal Society for the Prevention of Cruelty to Animals, and after investigating the case, the Society awarded Gyp his medal.

Peter Shaw Baker, Dog Heroes, 1935

Car Crash Hero

A SMART LITTLE mutt who proved his intelligence in a traffic accident was Shorty, half cocker spaniel and half Pekinese, owned by Mr and Mrs Ed Roach of Texarkana, Texas.

One day the Roaches and Shorty were in their car breezing along the highway between Wilton and DeQueen, Arkansas. Mr Roach was at the wheel, contentedly puffing on his pipe and keeping his eye on the road.

Mrs Roach and Shorty were looking out across the countryside, enjoying the ride. They made a picture of quiet happiness. No premonition of the tragedy just ahead troubled their minds. Then, with the suddenness of a lightning flash, it happened. Bang! A tyre blew, the car jumped out of control and went hurtling down the embankment and hit the bottom with a mighty crash.

Shorty was thrown out as it went down, but Mr and Mrs Roach were trapped and knocked unconscious. The burning pipe set fire to the upholstery. The embankment was so steep and the car had rolled so far that it could not be seen from the highway. Motorists sped by unaware of the tragedy below them.

Shorty ran to the wreck and saw his master and mistress lying in it with smoke and flames creeping near them. Something had to be done in a hurry, and he did it. He dashed up to the highway and started barking at every car that passed. Several drivers paid him no mind, thinking that he was just enjoying a little sport.

But luckily a man came along who understood dogs – C. E. Hendrix, a banker from Horatio, Arkansas. He could see Shorty was greatly disturbed, and wasn't barking at cars just for fun. He thought the dog was lost, as there was no house in sight, and wanted someone to take him home.

So Mr Hendrix stopped, opened the door of his car and called to the dog. But instead of coming toward him, Shorty started down the embankment. A moment later, though, he reappeared, barked again, and once more turned and disappeared. And Mr Hendrix got the idea. He was to follow. The dog wanted to show him something.

Mr Hendrix was shocked by the sight that greeted him. He saw he hadn't a moment to lose, for the fire was gaining. He pulled Mr and Mrs Roach out of the wreckage, and they were revived and taken to a doctor. Little Shorty's intelligence had saved their lives, and he was decorated.

Eldon Roarke, Just a Mutt, 1947

A Lifetime of Brilliance

A KEEPER called Hale – we are never told his first name – owned Bosun and the dog's brief period of fame, which came via the newspaper columns, was not brought about as a result of one particular act of intelligence but rather a lifetime of brilliance in the field.

The keeper told the newspaper that when he'd chosen Bosun as a puppy he had sensed there was something special about him. 'He was lively and had such a knowing look about him,' said Hale.

Bosun learned quickly to retrieve and was a star performer at every pheasant shoot, rarely failing to find a bird. He was also lightning quick. When Bosun was only eighteen months old, Hale was walking near the big house on the estate when he met a servant who explained that the house was in an uproar as the three-year-old daughter of the owners had gone missing. Her parents were frantic.

Having no certain idea that it would help, Hale offered to use Bosun to search for the child. A piece of the child's clothing was found, Bosun sniffed it and immediately set off with Hale close behind. Hale later said that it was as if Bosun had suddenly discovered he had a bloodhound gene in him.

The dog refused to be distracted from its mission as it criss-crossed a nearby wood moving gradually further away from the house. This continued for nearly an hour before the dog suddenly went into reverse and headed quickly back toward the house. A few hundred yards from home Bosun dived into an old ha-ha, or ditch. At the end of the ditch the little girl was found. She was fast asleep, scratched by brambles and covered in mud but otherwise unharmed. Bosun and Hale were greeted as heroes up at the house and Hale's wages were immediately increased. Word quickly spread of Bosun's extraordinary success and Hale was offered large sums of money for the dog – he refused and man and dog went back to their regular work.

Two years later Bosun managed another extraordinary feat. He'd gone to the local railway station with Hale to collect some rearing equipment that was arriving by train. While Hale passed the time of day with the stationmaster and other staff, Bosun curled up on the platform and went to sleep. Sometime later the train arrived and the rearing equipment was carried out to the waiting cart. It was then, as Hale got up behind the horses and prepared to set off for home, that he noticed Bosun was missing. He searched frantically around the station, the goods yard and around the fields beyond but there was no sign of the dog. This was extremely unusual, as Bosun had never been known to wander off before. As dusk fell Hale was forced to set off for home without the dog that had been his closest companion since he'd taken him home as a pup.

For several days there was no news at all in the district about the dog's fate but then an anonymous letter was pushed through the keeper's door. The writer claimed to have seen Bosun being dragged on to the train while Hale had been helping with the unloading. There was no way to verify this but Hale knew that the next station along the line was more than twenty miles away. On his next free day he caught the train, got off at the next stop and asked local shopkeepers and station staff if they'd seen Bosun. No one had set eyes on the missing dog and Hale was forced to return home once again alone.

It is easy to imagine his astonishment when, two days later, he received a message from the stationmaster telling him that Bosun had just jumped off the down train and was waiting sitting happily by the stationmaster's fire waiting for his master.

No one ever discovered if Bosun had simply escaped from his kidnappers and by sheer good luck hopped on a train going in the right direction to take him home. But whatever the answer this escapade added hugely to the dog's reputation in the locality.

Bosun's last great adventure came many years later near the end of his life. He'd never lost his enthusiasm for shooting and would always work until he was exhausted – so much so that Hale, who was not normally sentimental about animals, began to think the dog should be given less arduous work. He would never admit it but the old keeper was worried that Bosun might die on him. But Bosun would have none of it and when Hale left him at home on shoot days the dog looked so miserable that the keeper quickly gave in and started taking him out again.

Half way through Bosun's last season he was out with his master picking up as usual when a ferocious storm blew up and the final drive of the day had to be abandoned. The Guns made their way through an increasingly terrifying blizzard to a narrow lane where an estate cart was waiting for them. It was then that Hale noticed that the oldest of the Guns was missing. Hale set off back through the blizzard with Bosun at his heels to find the man.

Visibility was poor by now as the light began to fail and the snowstorm grew increasingly violent. Hale checked along the line of the last drive but failed to see the old man. With no idea what else to try he tried to encourage Bosun out ahead of him to look. The dog seemed to grasp what was wanted almost immediately and set off on a line away from the ride where the last drive had taken place and into the wood.

Within minutes and despite the terrible storm he had found the old man. He had failed to see the others leaving and was quickly lost when the snow began to fall. He'd taken shelter under the trees and having no idea which direction might lead him to safety he had begun seriously to consider the possibility that he might die. When Hale told him that Bosun had found him virtually unaided the old man could hardly believe his ears. Just a few months later Bosun died in his sleep, probably from a heart attack.

Peter Jensen, *High Days and Holidays*, 1922

Tank Busters

DURING WORLD WAR II the Germans, British, Russians and Japanese all trained dogs to help with the war effort but the different attitudes to animals in each country can best be judged by the fact that the Russians and the Japanese used half-starved dogs that were sent out carrying bombs – effectively these were dog suicide bombers. The British were too fond of their dogs even to contemplate such an idea.

The Russians probably trained more dogs than anyone – some 50,000 dogs were recruited or bred specifically for the purpose before and during the war. They were used to attack the enemy or to discover the enemy's position but mostly to rescue injured soldiers who, in the dreadful Russian winter, were likely to die from exposure rather than their wounds if they were not rescued quickly. Dogs were much faster through the snow than horses or vehicles and when they found a man they were trained to lie next to him to try to keep him warm till help arrived.

The Russians awarded a number of special medals to their dogs – these included the Order of Bagdan Khmelnitsky, the Order of the Red Star and the Order of Alexander Nevsky.

Alsatians – or German Shepherds – were most often used for rescue work while pure white Samoyeds were excellent for winter attacks. They would pull Russian marksmen (dressed in white) on sleds towards the enemy lines – they could move silently and were almost invisible until it was too late for the enemy to react.

Russian suicide dogs were trained to search for food under tanks – they would be released when enemy tanks were in sight and had special armour busting bombs attached to their backs. They would run towards the enemy tanks and then dash about underneath the enemy tanks until a special pressure trigger exploded the bomb which cut through the underside of the tank.

There are many examples of the success of these suicide anti-tank dogs – at Izyum for example they are said to have been so effective that as soon as the Germans heard barking they turned their tanks and fled.

But it was not all plain sailing – according to some reports the dogs sometimes got confused and ran back under their own tanks and destroyed them.

The Japanese were probably the least effective in using dogs – they knew so little about training dogs that they thought harsh methods would work best. In fact the dogs were hopeless simply because they responded more to American gestures of friendliness than to their Japanese masters' blows.

Tom Quinn, *Shooting's Strangest Days*, 2002

Dog Saves Man

WILDFOWLING WAS and is one of Britain's most dangerous sports. It is not the shotguns that cause the problems but rather the remote places where wildfowlers enjoy their sport.

A copy of a long vanished Norfolk newspaper published in 1900 records a story that almost led to the death of a wildfowler – in fact the story is a reminder of the perils of shooting on mudflats at low tide where even the most experienced shot can get into serious difficulties.

The paper records that the fowler had set off early in the morning to a stretch of foreshore where he had shot regularly for years. What the fowler hadn't realised was that work on a number of sea defences further up the coast had changed the mud landscape.

Several freezing hours later he had bagged a couple of mallard and decided to call it a day. He began the long march back across the sticky mud knowing that he had at least a thirty minute safety margin before his retreat would be cut off by the incoming tide. But he had reckoned without those changes up the coast. He reached a gully that would normally have been dry at this time of day and was horrified to discover deep swirling water cutting him off from the distant sand dunes.

He ran wildly along the edge of the gully ever more desperate and seeing no way to cross the water that was rising higher with every passing second.

Then on the distant sandy shore he saw a Labrador. He shouted and waved hoping that the Labrador might attract the attention of his owner but instead the dog simply stopped and stared across at him. This went on for some time but then the dog did something extraordinary. It plunged into the water and began swimming towards the stranded fowler. A few minutes later it clambered up the side of the muddy gully, shook itself and began nuzzling his leg.

The stranded fowler stared back across the gully hoping to catch a glimpse of the dog's owner, but the beach and distant dunes were deserted.

The dog began to whine and looked as if it wanted to get back to the shore. Whenever the fowler ignored it, the dog began to whine. By now there was little chance of surviving long enough in the water to make the shore if he risked dying of cold by swimming, but his other options had all vanished. Then he had an idea. He left his gun and bag, his boots and cartridge bag and his heavy waterproofs on the ground and walked to the edge of the gully with the dog. He grabbed its collar and urged it into the water. Within seconds the dog was pulling strongly for the shore with the wildfowler hanging on to its collar and kicking with his legs as hard as he could. But the water was so cold that within a minute he had become completely numb; he began to feel sleepy and was in danger of giving up so terrible was the cold. But each time his determination flagged the dog barked loudly as if willing him to keep trying. Moments later they reached the beach and the wildfowler was able to stagger half a mile to the nearest house. Without the help of the dog he would certainly have died but when he had dried himself, warmed up and was ready to head for home he asked the couple who had helped him if they had seen the dog that had accompanied him. They shook their heads and told him he had been alone when he reached their cottage. From that day on the wildfowler wondered whose dog had saved him but he never found out and he never saw the dog again.

Country Times, March 1980

Boar Battle

THE STORY OF how Bruce, a Great Dane belonging to Mr G. Davis, of Bradfield Farm, won his animal Victoria Cross Collar will be told and re-told for many years to come by the inhabitants of the little Essex village of Doddinghurst.

His hour-long battle with the boar is an epic which will not easily be forgotten by those who witnessed it. Any reader who cares to visit either of the village's two little inns of an evening when the farm hands are forgathered, will find little difficulty in discovering one who will be willing to tell him the tale.

For did not the cries and snarls of that battle royal echo throughout the whole village and out beyond, so that the labourers at work in the fields dropped their tools and hurried down, to discover the cause of all the commotion?

It happened one afternoon in June 1934. The village lay wrapped in silence. The men folk were away in the fields at their work, their women were taking a well-earned siesta. A sense of serene peace and quietness enveloped the entire countryside. The only travellers along the dusty white road that curled through the village were white and brown butterflies fluttering idly with the light breeze. It was a warm breeze, laden with the scents of summer, and carried with it the sounds of the fields and meadows – an indistinct murmur of insects on the wing, the rustle of the air itself among the leaves of the oaks and elms, the call of a thrush or greenfinch, the chirrup of grasshoppers, the faint tremor o'er earth and air as a horse shook itself – these and a dozen other sounds blended into one throb – the throb of life itself. Steady, measured and never ceasing.

The only sound that gave evidence of human activity was a distant drone and clatter, telling of a meadow, hidden from sight by a fold in the land, being mowed.

A great expanse of green meadows and ploughed furrow enclosed the sleepy village. The neat line of the hedges bounding the road and the fields was broken here and there by groups of heavily-massed trees, behind which white, billowy clouds rolled together in the sky.

At Bradfield Farm all was still and silent. In the farmyard, the fowls had left off scratching in search of insects, and lay basking in the afternoon sun, in little spaces hollowed out by their feet and wings as they shook the dust up into their feathers.

In the shadow of the long cowshed, lay Bruce, the

Great Dane, hero of this story. His massive head rested on his forepaws, and his ears twitched occasionally to drive away the flies that settled there. A heavy chain was fastened to his collar, and to a staple in the wall.

As he lay resting, a shrill scream shattered the quiet and peace of the summer's afternoon, sending the great dog in one bound to his feet, ears and tail erect, nostrils quivering. Again that scream – a terrified scream of a woman in distress – quivered through the stillness of the afternoon. The Great Dane stretched at the length of his chain, straining in the direction whence the sound came. A moment later a woman, her hair streaming, her face flushed and anxious, ran at full tilt round the corner of the line of cowsheds. Close at her heels followed a large white boar, his huge body swaying from side to side as he raced after the woman, his small feet covering the ground at an amazing rate. The woman's foot caught in a cobble, she stumbled, grasped for support at a door of the cowshed which stood open, and managed to save herself from falling.

But the delay had brought the boar up to her heels. She stumbled forward again, gasping painfully for breath and exerting all that remained of her spent energy to reach the house and escape the tusks of the half-mad creature at her heels.

Meanwhile, Bruce had added his voice to the hubbub. Recognizing the woman instantly as his mistress, he appreciated the danger that threatened her. But the heavy chain held him back from rendering the assistance he could otherwise have given. Again and again he hurled his great body forward, only to have it jerked back when the chain ran taut. His neck hurt where the collar tugged at it, and the sudden jerks jolted the breath out of his body, but he took no heed and hurled himself forward again. He leapt, was checked for an instant in mid-air by the chain, and then plunged forward, rolling over in a heap on the cobblestones; the chain was still attached to his collar, but the staple in the wall to which it had been fixed had been pulled out by the force of the jump. Scrambling to his feet, he bounded across the yard, the chain dragging over the stones behind him.

Then commenced a battle that was to last for what seemed like an hour. The dog had the advantage of height and agility, but the boar had greater weight, and its tough hide left few vulnerable spots. The dog was hampered, too, by the chain dangling from his collar. The first rush the dog made took the boar by surprise – he was too intent on his quarry to notice the dog.

Bruce rushed at him, a vexed grumble rolling in his throat, and sought to grip him at the back of the neck. His teeth found their hold in the folds of thick skin, and, closing his jaws, he tugged with all his strength.

With a snort in which astonishment mingled with rage, the boar swung its body round to meet this unexpected attack, the dog swung with him, and thrice they circled completely round, neither quite determined what to do next.

Then the dog, realizing that to retain his hold would only sap his strength whilst not seriously affecting that of his opponent, released his grip and leapt back. In a flash he was forward again, reaching out to seize the boar's huge snout. But he was not quite quick enough; the boar threw its head up, and one of its long tusks struck the dog on the side of the jaw, sending him reeling sideways.

Bruce drew back. He was not afraid – there was no place for fear in his heart – but he recognized in his adversary a skilled fighter, one whose abilities must be respected.

He decided to adopt other tactics. Darting from side to side, he barked furiously at the boar, first in this ear and then in that, confusing it by the noise he made, muddling its mind by his rapid movements. Then, seizing his opportunity, he grabbed at one of his enemy's long ears.

The boar screeched with pain and impotent rage, and whirled around in a vain effort to shake itself free. Round and round they whirled, tumbling over one another, blind to everything else except their mutual desire to kill one another.

A cloud of white dust rose above them, the fowls flew in terror from the yard, cackling loudly in protest at this disturbance of the afternoon peace. Some rooks, resting in the upper branches of a group of nearby elms, flew out in alarm, the ducks on the little pond adjoining the farmyard gathered in an anxious group, and quacked to one another plaintively.

The whole scene, so quiet and peaceful a short while earlier, now echoed with cries of alarm and distress, above which the screech of the boar and the angry deep-throated snarls of the dog predominated. Several women from nearby cottages hurried to the scene; some children, so small that even school had no use for them yet, raced excitedly from the far end of the village, a mare in the meadow beyond the cowsheds neighed, calling her foal to her side. And still the fight continued.

Once, the dog missed his footing, and was crushed against the wall. He felt the hot, foul breath from the boar's nostrils fan his face, saw its wicked, beady eyes glaring relentlessly into his own, and then one of the tusks sank deep into the flesh of his neck.

Somehow he managed to break free and scramble to his feet again. For over an hour the battle raged with unabated fury. Farm hands from the fields arrived on the scene, for the uproar of the conflict could be heard nearly a mile away. They tried to separate the pair, but in vain. Right across the yard, past the stables and into the little garden in front of the farmhouse the pair fought.

Rose trees, delphiniums and Canterbury bells scattered in all directions, but neither animal took any heed; each had its eyes fixed relentlessly on the other's, each was fired with but one desire – the desire to kill.

Bruce, strong though he was, felt his strength beginning to ebb; the continual knocks and blows he received dazed his mind, and the chain trailing from his collar kept entangling itself in his legs, making him stumble and falter when he tried to leap away from those terrible tusks.

His sight became blurred, and his muscles answered the messages flashed to them a fraction of a second too late.

Then he saw the opportunity for which he had been waiting for nearly an hour. The boar lunged at him, its snout passed within a few inches of his mouth ... he seized it in his jaws as it swung past, and held it fast. The boar swung this way and that, banging the dog's head down on the ground again and again, half stunning him. But though his brain reeled, and the brilliant sunlight faded into dim darkness, the dog held on; through his confused brain there ran one clear thought – never, never, happen what may, must he let go of that snout.

The end came at last. The boar, overwhelmed by pain and exhaustion, rolled over on its flank, and lay quivering. Several of the men who had hurried to the scene, rushed forward to seize Bruce. Dimly aware that victory was his, he released his hold, and allowed them to carry his battered body away.

The trouble had all started when Mrs Davis went into the meadow to feed a sow and her litter of young porkers. The boar – a large four-year-old Middle White – was kept shut up in the barn because it was so vicious, but it had somehow managed to work its way out, and as soon as it saw her approach the sow, rushed at her furiously, chasing her right across the meadow and into the yard.

Bruce, who usually has the free run of the farm, was kept chained up at that time because he was inclined to worry the young pigs. The dog is a fine specimen of his breed; he has a quiet dignity and an air of self-reliance which is very pleasing to observe.

Every summer a number of children from the slums of the East End of London come to spend their holidays at a free camp established by Mr Davis on the farm.

Bruce enjoys their company, and is a great favourite with them. He lets the youngsters take any number of liberties with him. During the winter months, he often goes round collecting money to help pay for the children's holiday.

Peter Shaw Baker, *Dog Heroes*, 1935

Well Trained

Lousy, owned by the Lafayette Williamses of Fredericksburg, Virginia won his silver medal for saving the life of a good friend of his, George Ball, a telegraph operator at the Hamilton's Crossing tower.

Mr Ball had been with the railroad thirty-two years, twenty of them at the tower. It was his habit to park his car, climb a fence and take a shortcut to and from his post. That was his routine, winter and summer.

One foul, sleety night in December, 1911, with the thermometer registering 'minus 5 below,' Mr Ball left the tower shortly after midnight and started home. As he attempted to climb the ice-covered fence, he slipped and fell, suffering a compound fracture of the leg.

Lying on the frozen ground, writhing in agony he would never have been able to get off the tracks before the next train came along if it hadn't been for Lousy who first tried pulling Mr Ball off the track by the sleeve and then by his jacket front.

When that failed Lousy sprinted off to get help. He pestered and pestered a group of passers-by until, intrigued, they followed him to the railway where they were just in time to pull Mr Ball clear of a thundering freight train. Lousy needless to say was the toast of the town, his deed written up in newspapers across the state and even in newspapers in far away New York.

Eldon Roarke, *Just a Mutt*, 1947

Chapter Three

SPORTING

Dog Gone

Sʜᴏᴏᴛɪɴɢ ᴊᴜsᴛ wouldn't be the same without a dog. Out on the marsh or at a peg on a pheasant drive, a dog is a partner in the shooting process as well as being an excellent companion. For many shooting men life without a dog is unthinkable.

The Victorian writer John Guille Millais was often far more interested in the antics of his shooting dog than in the shooting for which he'd bought the dog in the first place. This passion for all things canine reached dizzying heights after one extraordinary day on the Tay.

Millais had downed a goose that crashed into the sea. His dog launched itself into the icy waves in pursuit. The dog vanished into the frozen distance. And it took Millais some time even to locate it using his telescope.

Millais grew increasingly concerned as the tiny distant dot began to fade from view. He ran along the foreshore desperately looking for a boat and after about a mile was lucky enough to come across a bait digger prepared to part with his boat for half an hour – in return for a fee. Rowing through the blinding freezing spray cannot have been easy but Millais was nothing if not determined and he refused to give up even as the shore began to recede and still no sign of his beloved dog.

A good way out in the estuary he shouted and called to the dog but there was no response. Then he spotted a tiny black head in the distance. By now he was a mile out. He was astonished to discover his dog still carrying the heavy goose he'd shot and refusing to drop it despite the impossibility of getting back to shore. She was quite clearly prepared to die rather than give up and one can only imagine Millais' delight when he finally pulled her into the boat – still refusing to let go of the goose.

Art and Sport, 1936

Seal of Approval

Until well into the twentieth century visitors to Scotland and the West Country of England often went seal shooting. Such sport would be frowned on now but a century and more ago seal numbers were high and local fishermen believed the seals took too many fish and were very happy to see them shot.

The technique was to shoot them with a rifle but in such a way that the dead seal didn't sink. The best way to do this was to shoot the seal on land but the difficulty was that often even a mortally wounded seal had enough energy to throw itself into the water where it immediately sank and was unrecoverable. Occasionally, for reasons no one could quite make out, a seal would fall into the water and not sink. In these cases the shooter would often set off in a rowing boat to retrieve the seal but with the fast tides that poured through the rock channels off the North coast of Scotland this could be a tricky operation.

On one remarkable day – according to a report that later appeared in a local newspaper – what should have been a tricky operation almost turned into a tragedy.

It began when an English sportsman shot a seal that seemed to be well back from the water's edge. Unfortunately the seal had enough life left in it to reach the sea where it dived and vanished. Cursing his luck the man who had fired the shot was considering packing up for home when, moments later, the seal floated to the surface. It was certainly dead but already a couple of hundred yards from the shore.

He set off over the rocks towards the boat that was kept in a small boat house at a point where a small stream entered the sea. Luckily the boat was moored in precisely the direction in which the seal was drifting.

Just as he reached the boat the man realised his spaniel was missing. He ran back over the rocks shouting and whistling but no sign of her. He thought she had probably gone off in search of rabbits but this was not like her at all.

Assuming she was safe and determined to bring back the seal he launched the boat and began rowing furiously out to sea and toward the now distant speck of seal. He was probably half a mile from the shore when he stopped rowing and checked the position of the seal through his binoculars. He then noticed a tiny flurry at the side of the seal as if it were being attacked by a small shoal of fish.

He began rowing again and was soon close enough to get a really good look at the seal and, to his astonishment, he saw clinging to the seal's neck his cocker spaniel. She was dwarfed by the seal but had clearly decided that she would try to retrieve it and despite the fact that she had now drifted almost a mile offshore she was still determined not to let go! On reaching the seal he pulled the dog aboard by the scruff of the neck and then roped the seal's tail to the back of the boat. Against the tide it was a long exhausting journey back to the shore pulling the heavy seal. The dog slumped exhausted in the well of the boat and he realised that if he had not caught up with the seal the dog would certainly have continued to hold on until she drowned from exhaustion so determined was she to retrieve what her master had shot.

R.S.V. Williams, *Sport for All*, 1909

Mack Down a Hole

IF EVER A dog used his head, Mack did. Mack was a pointer, owned by B. Buchanan, Junior. One Christmas day Mr Buchanan decided he'd like to do a little shooting, so he and his dog drove out into the country.

He parked the car, and they struck out across a field. Mack was feeling good. He was just a white streak going through the sagebrush. Mr Buchanan couldn't keep up with Mack when the pointer felt like that, and in a few minutes the dog had disappeared.

But Mr Buchanan didn't worry because that happened all the time. Mack would disappear, and then Mr Buchanan would look for him – and find him pointing birds, standing like a marble statue.

Now Mr Buchanan trudged along, looking around. But no Mack. Then he started circling. But still no Mack. Fear began to grip Mr Buchanan, and he quickened his pace. And then from somewhere – apparently far in the distance – came a faint yelping and whining.

Mr Buchanan stopped – and listened. No, that wasn't Mack. That was some farmer's dog. He walked on. The whining grew louder. It did sound a little like Mack. But it couldn't be. It was too far away. Suddenly – almost before he realized it – he was right over the yelping and whining. Trembling with fear and excitement, he pushed through a clump of tall sagebrush – and stood on the brink of a great yawning hole! Mack was down in the bottom of it – ten feet down in an old cistern, swimming for dear life.

As Mr Buchanan leaned over and spoke words of encouragement to his dog – 'Take it easy, old fella, I'll get you out' – an awful stench jabbed him in the nose, and he saw the bloated bodies of small animals in the water. Something had to be done quickly, for Mr Buchanan could see that the frantic dog was near collapse.

He looked across the fields in all directions, but help was nowhere in sight. Then it popped into his mind that there was just one chance, one thing to do. He pulled off his clothes – every stitch except his shorts. He tied his shirt, undershirt and pants together, and then he made a loop with his belt and tied that to the end of his clothes-rope. Quickly he lowered it and started fishing. But he couldn't get that loop over Mack's head.

Although he was practically naked, out in an open field on Christmas day, Mr Buchanan began to sweat a little. It's an awful thing for a man to stand only ten feet away from his dog and see him die, powerless to help him.

All at once the improvised rope stiffened! Mack had the other end of it in his mouth, swinging to the pants leg.

'Atta boy, Mack! Hold on, old fella!'

Mr Buchanan started pulling up, exerting all his will-power to keep from going too fast and pulling with jerks.

'Hold on, Mack! Just a little more now, just a little more,' he begged. And Mack, breathing hard, the muscles of his jaws quivering, hung on. 'Good boy! Out we ...'

Mack's strong jaws suddenly gave way just as he reached the top, and down he plunged with a mighty splash. He came up whimpering, pleading. Hope and fear hammered at each other in Mr Buchanan's brain. Hope – maybe Mack would catch hold and swing on again. He had never been trained to hold things in his mouth, to swing on to sacks or sticks. He was a hunting dog... none of that play stuff for him.

But he was smart. Maybe he would. But Mack was getting weaker fast. If he couldn't hold on long enough the first time, he couldn't the second. Mr Buchanan clutched the rope tightly and kept his voice calm. 'Catch it again, Mack. Grab hold, old fella.'

He had it! Once more Mr Buchanan began pulling up –
swiftly but steadily. 'We'll make it this time … Hold tight!
Hold tight!'

Mack's neck stretched and looked as if it were about
to be pulled right out of his shoulders, but he clamped his
jaws all the tighter. And then he got his forepaws over the
top of the cistern! Mr Buchanan grabbed him. They had
made it! The dog was so groggy from exhaustion and fear
that he could hardly stand. Mr Buchanan quickly unknot-
ted the makeshift rope and dressed. Then he wrapped
Mack in his hunting coat and carried him a mile to the car.

Eldon Roarke, *Just a Mutt*, 1947

Sleeping Partner

WHERE WOULD we be without our dogs? Half the pleasure of shooting is the companionship of a good dog –
which may explain why many of us are happy to spend
a small fortune on a top quality Labrador or spaniel.
Most dogs will keep working until they drop, but there
are numerous hilarious – and occasionally extraordinary
– stories of dogs who decided it was really time they did
their own thing.

One of the most famous shooting dog stories concerned a splendid animal owned by a close friend of
King Edward VII. Not wanting to be disgraced by a poor

animal in such illustrious company, the king's friend made sure he bought the best dog that money could buy: it was fully trained and came from a long line of excellent gun-dogs. Its new owner was assured that it would behave impeccably yet on its first day in the field the dog vanished almost as soon as the first drive had begun. It pricked up its ears at the sound of the beaters and disappeared into the nearest woodland.

The dog re-appeared at lunchtime and re-joined its master as if nothing had happened until the shooting started again in the afternoon. Then it disappeared again and despite a great deal of searching it could not be found until about three o'clock when the final shots died away and the last drive came to an end.

Loathe to give up on a dog with such a fine pedigree, the owner took it to other shoots where his fellow Guns were less exalted. But wherever they went precisely the same thing happened and the dog, once gone, could never be found.

At last by sheer good fortune the dog's secret was dis-covered. A beater who had stayed well behind the other beaters after hurting his foot saw a dog creeping through the field the beaters had just crossed and dropping into a nearby ditch. The beater hobbled over and found the dog curled up, fast asleep and snoring loudly. And there it slept until some sixth sense told it lunch was in the offing at which time it woke up and headed back to its master.

After this discovery numerous attempts were made to curb the dog's terrible habit but all failed. Kept on a leash and attached to the Gun's peg the dog showed every interest in proceedings but as soon as it was turned loose to retrieve a bird it immediately ran off and could only rarely be found. Soon the owner gave up and kept the dog as a pet so while other dogs worked hard in all weathers for their keep this crafty animal stayed permanently at home curled up in front of the fire.

The Gamekeeper, 1903

Trouting Labrador

AN ELDERLY shooting man who was still a regular at the local shoot well into his nineties, always insisted on taking two or three dogs with him. The dogs seemed almost as ancient as he was himself and one of them – the old man's favourite – had lost the use of its back legs. Nothing daunted the old man had commissioned a blacksmith friend to make a set of lightweight wheels attached to two shafts that were strapped to the dog's back. After initial problems the dog got the idea and began to race about again like a puppy. Its owner quickly realised that the dog's retrieving abilities would be even further enhanced if the wheels were fitted with a suspension system. Once again the blacksmith got to work and soon the dog was winning an occasional local retrieving competition as well as picking up regularly on local shoots. The old man was delighted and the dog led an active life far beyond what would normally be expected for a Labrador.

The old man was clearly something of an eccentric because in addition to building wheels for one Labrador he taught another to retrieve not birds or rabbits or hares but fish.

The technique was simple. The old man would hook a trout and play it until it was almost ready for the net. Then, instead of using a net, he would whistle to his dog and it would dive into the river, grab the fish and leap out delivering it neatly to hand. The old man insisted it saved him the back breaking business of carrying a net and it gave the Labrador plenty of exercise. But there were drawbacks. Eventually the dog insisted on waiting in the river rather than on the bank until its master had hooked a fish and it became hopeless at retrieving birds!

E. W. Edwards, *Thoughts on Fishing*, 1926

Bosun's Antics

THE AVON below Salisbury was a wonderful mixed fishery until abstraction and pollution reduced water levels and water quality. Now the great shoals of sleek grayling and butter-coloured trout are largely gone, although coarse fish remain in reduced numbers. Somehow, despite reassuring noises from the scientists about water quality, the river no longer sparkles.

But back in the 1960s the fishing could be fabulous and an occasional salmon was even taken.

An elderly fisherman who came down every Wednesday to fish The London Anglers Association water always came with his old black Labrador. The old man was unusual in that he was a keen coarse fisherman who, when he thought conditions were right, fished the fly. He always put his coarse fish back as gently as possible, but any trout unlucky enough to be seduced by his fly was taken home for supper.

Other fishermen always noticed that when the old man hooked a fish his dog became wildly excited, jumping and almost turning somersaults until the fish was in the net. One day another regular got chatting to the old man and commented on the antics of his dog.

'Oh, he thinks I'm going to send him to get the fish,' said the old man. 'I used to fish on a very difficult water where you'd hook a fish and he'd tear off into a thick weed bed from which he could only rarely be extracted. When Bosun here was a puppy I gradually taught him to swim out to this weed bed and either swim down and grab the fish while it was still on the hook or, if he couldn't do that, at least try to move the fish out of the weeds. Nine times out of ten it worked wonderfully well and I caught a lot more fish than I would have otherwise. But then we moved and I no longer fished that river. I got a ticket for this water and, so far, I've never had to call on Bosun's services. As you can see he gets pretty cross about it!'

The young man listened to the old fellow talking and assumed he was being teased so he nodded, said good morning and walked off to fish a distant meadow.

'I think he's lost his marbles,' he mumbled to himself and thought nothing more of it. Then two weeks later he happened to be crossing one of the carriers – the man-made streams that criss-cross the old water meadows below Salisbury – when he spotted the old man again. From the look of his rod the old man had hooked a good fish and since it was quite clearly a fly rod it must be a big trout or a small salmon.

The younger man thought the least he could do was wander along and offer to net the fish for the old man, and he was half way across the intervening meadow when he noticed the dog running away from the old man. Then in an instant he saw the dog turn – almost as a bowler turns towards the wicket before beginning his run – and dash towards the water. The dog flew into the air and landed in the carrier about half way across with a huge splash. The dog glanced above him continually as he swam across; then as he neared a thick overhanging willow he ducked under the water and vanished from sight. Minutes seemed to pass and then the dog reappeared with a trout in its mouth and a very fine trout it was too.

The dog arrived on the bank and presented the trout to its master as if it were a pheasant. When the younger man finally came up to the old man the fish – which looked as if it weighed about two pounds – had been unhooked and stowed away in the old man's knapsack.

'I must admit I didn't believe a word of it when you told me about your dog,' said the young man as he came up to the old fisherman.

'Quite all right,' came the reply, 'it does sound like a bit of a tall story, but Bosun has landed hundreds of fish like that. I'm only sad he doesn't get the chance more often. That's why he jumps around so much – it's as if he's asking me to go and fish somewhere I'm more likely to get snagged up!'

And with that he whistled up the dog and wandered away.

Tom Quinn, *Fish Tales*, 1992

Hair of the Dog

A FAMOUS GILLIE who's worked on the Spey for dec-
ades used regularly to catch fish when others found it
extremely difficult or impossible. Some put it down to
his enormous experience while others thought it was just
that the gillie knew the water so well he could time his
fishing to perfection.

One day in the early 1970s he'd done particularly well
each time his guest handed him the rod and went off for
a while. When the fisherman returned he found that the
gillie had landed another fish. After three fish had been
landed in this way the fisherman decided to stick it out.
He fished hard for a couple of hours. Nothing. It was
puzzling because the fisherman was experienced and
extremely knowledgeable. Eventually he stopped fishing,
offered the gillie a dram from his flask and asked him how
he did it.

Feeling sorry for the fisherman who was an old friend,
the gillie looked about quickly and then beckoned the
fisherman to come closer.

'Dog hair,' said the gillie.

'What!' said the fisherman.

'Dog hair,' came the reply.

'What on earth has dog hair got to do with it?'

'Each time you went away I tied a bit of my old
Alsatian's fur to the hook. On a dour day like this it can

make all the difference.' The fisherman clearly didn't believe a word of it so the gillie took the rod, reeled in and having fished around in his pocket tied on a short tuft of blackish hair. Five minutes later he was into a good fish.

The fisherman was astonished. This time instead of removing the dog hair when he handed the rod back to the fisherman the gillie left it on and within minutes another salmon lay on the bank.

The gillie insisted the trick did not always work, but when everything else had been tried it was, he said, always worth a shot.

Tom Quinn, *Tales from the Water's Edge*, 1992

Fish Retriever

Romney Marsh is one of the loneliest most windswept regions of Britain. Here sheep have grazed for more than a thousand years and along the many drainage channels, creeks and inlets smugglers once brought their contraband ashore. But Romney Marsh is also an excellent place for the pike fisher. Here miles of water are home to some

of the best pike in Britain. They grow fat on the teem-
ing roach and rudd that breed prolifically throughout the
waterways.

One bright winter's morning two friends cast their
pike baits into a deep channel at the extreme end of the
freshwater section just a few hundred yards from the
more brackish water where there was a good chance of
catching a flounder or a mullet.

For the first hour the two big bright pike floats bobbed
about with not a sign of a fish. The two men lost interest as
the icy wind gradually numbed them. They left their baits
fishing and wandered off with their dogs at heel to try to
warm up. Returning some ten minutes later they discovered that one rod had disappeared. At first they thought it
might have been stolen, but that seemed unlikely in such
a remote spot.

Then one of the two men spotted the missing pike
float far away down the river. They gave chase, and having
caught up with the float realised that somewhere down in
the water beneath it was a pike that had hooked itself. But
this was a wide river and there was no way to reach the
float. Then twenty yards upstream of the float they saw
the rod. There was only one thing to do. They shouted
'Fetch!' to the better of the two dogs and in an instant
the big Labrador was powering through the water. When
it reached the rod, the Labrador grabbed the rod's cork
handle and turned for the shore. It swam a few feet but

was then unceremoniously tugged in the opposite direction. The pike was being played by the Labrador.

Now this was a dog that did not like to give up. It had swum much bigger, colder rivers than this and having been told to bring this curiously lively stick to its master it was determined to do it come what may. Thus began a twenty minute battle between a very determined Labrador and a very determined pike. At the end of that time the Labrador managed to reach the bank. Luckily it was a bank that shelved gradually away and the Labrador, having backed out of the water kept hold of the rod and continued to back up until the pike came bouncing on to the shore. The fish – probably the only fish ever to be played and landed by a Labrador – weighed eleven pounds.

The one slightly unfortunate result of the whole affair was that the dog developed a taste for fishing. Whenever its owner hooked a fish from then on, the dog would bark and howl until the fish had been landed or until he had been given the rod so he could land the fish. On quiet, expensive fisheries the noise of the fish-mad dog became such an embarrassment that the fisherman often had to leave the dog at home. But in the remaining six years of its life the fishing Labrador managed to land several more pike as well as a number of trout, two eels and a three pound chub.

A.J.T. Matlock, *River of Dreams*, 1938

Chapter Four

SENTIMENTAL

Moustache

A FRENCH MILITARY officer, known to a friend of mine, had a poodle, who had been his companion for years, and had frequently slept with him on the battlefield.

Moustache had been taught by his master to fetch provisions as they were wanted from any place near to his quarters. The poodle acquitted himself with such sagacity, that it reached the ears of many of the officers; and one day, when Moustache was the bearer of a note and a basket for some fowls from a farmhouse above a mile distant, they determined to watch his movements, which they reported as follows.

The fowls asked for were put alive into the basket, which had two lids, and were borne along safely by Moustache as he went on his way; but when he set the basket on the ground, that he might rest, one of the fowls lifted a lid of the basket, and got out, intent on making its way homewards.

But vain were its efforts; the poodle, carefully watching his charge, pursued the wanderer, brought it back, and pushing up the basket-lid with his nose, returned it to its prison. While, however, he was doing this, a fowl on the opposite side of the basket became alarmed, and tried to decamp; when Moustache caught and replaced it in the same manner.

Again and again did a rest bring on this singular trouble, fowl after fowl escaping and requiring to be caught; and at length Moustache was seen to pause, and evidently to be putting on his 'considering cap'.

In a moment he made up his mind: catching the fowl that had last got out of the basket, he gave it a gripe in the neck, placed it in the basket dead, and as the others got out in succession, served each one the same way, when he took up his charge and hurried home to his master, to the great astonishment as well as amusement of all who witnessed these very singular exploits.

Among Moustache's amusing tricks was one of playing the deserter.

With dropped tail and ears, going through his trial; imprisoned in a corner on his conviction; when brought out for execution, standing upright to be shot at; and at the sound imitating the discharge of guns, suddenly falling down, and lying stretched out on the floor as if he were actually dead.

A large sum was offered for Moustache to his master, by an officer of high rank, for his purchase, but it was declined; the dog was too highly valued to be parted with on any terms. Shortly after, some miscreant poisoned the dog. His master deeply felt the loss, and years after, when Moustache was mentioned, could scarcely refrain from tears.

Francis Jackman, *Journeyman*, 1867

Pilot Scheme

OUR PROPERTY was in a lonely dangerous place subject to burglaries and occasional violent attack and there must be protection in my absences. So we sought for a dog, and Pilot was sent to us. I knew his reputation was not good, as far as the law was concerned, for he had bitten a rates collector and followed that up by biting the policeman who had called to inquire as to whether it was true that he had bitten the rates collector, and when the postman had been laughing about this as a great joke, he bit him also.

This happened in a town many miles distant from Charters Towers, and the story of Pilot was conveyed to a friend of mine by letter. This friend told me that the lady who owned Pilot had been ordered by the court magistrate to get rid of the dog. He assured me that he had been bred and reared by this lady, and was really as gentle as a lamb but as brave as a lion, and all this talk of biting people was ridiculous and unfortunate.

The big point was, that the magistrate had not said that the dog must be destroyed. He may have meant that, but he had distinctly said: 'You must get rid of that dog within a week.'

We talked it all over, and a telegram was sent to the lady, with the result that Pilot was sent to us. He was evidently either a sheep-dog or a cattle-dog, of medium size, black coat with tan legs and muzzle, and a beautiful light in his eyes which combined mischief and courage. He fell in love with my wife at once, and his love was responded to without stint. Me he tolerated as a necessary nuisance.

I had come home in the early hours of the morning from the newspaper office and had disturbed my wife, who had been fast asleep.

She made a sign for me to sit quietly, and she pointed to Pilot who was lying at her feet. He was lying with head erect, and nose pointed in the direction of the bedroom, waiting. Presently the baby cry came again, this time sharper and more insistent. The dog now rose to his feet, and looked into my wife's eyes, but she made no sign, so he marched through the door, down the passage and into the bedroom.

Now came a series of sharp cries from master baby, who knew exactly what note to use when he thought his Mother should come more quickly. This was followed by the patter of feet, and Pilot stood in the doorway, the picture of indignation.

My wife went on with her reading, as if nothing was happening, and then there came from the dog a series of whines. No notice was taken, so he repeated the signal more insistently. Then came the baby cry again – not a cry with tears, but just the signal of a child insisting on the presence of someone.

Now Pilot lost all patience, and coming forward he sat at my wife's feet, and, looking into her eyes, tapped her knee time after time with his foot, and whined, as much as to say: 'You must come – you certainly must.'

Having shown me just what Pilot did regularly every night when the baby raised his voice, my wife rose to go to the bedroom, and the dog turned circles and wagged his tail and showed his teeth in a smile of delight, and reaching the cradle first, stood vigorously wagging his tail as she lifted the child into her arms.

If set to guard the baby he never moved until taken off duty, and woe to anything, human or otherwise, which came near the sleeping child. Once a fowl, innocently picking up bits, lost her head in a very decided fashion as she stopped to pick up something from under the baby carriage in the yard. Each of our two nanny goats lost a piece of an ear, because they imagined that they could come and eat something connected with the same baby carriage, when his majesty the baby was asleep.

No tradesman came into the yard while Pilot was on duty, and the idea of using our grounds as a thoroughfare was unanimously and enthusiastically abandoned by all who had once met our dog.

There was one man who must have been driven to despair by Pilot's vigilance. We discovered all about him afterwards, but at the time it was a very trying and rather baffling experience for us. It began one night after I had left home for the office, and my wife was sitting with Pilot in the dining room, which had a latticed end, so that she might enjoy the cool air after a blazing day.

Presently she heard Pilot growling very quietly, and that was a certain sign that someone was approaching the house. She became alert and watchful, and the dog now lay quietly with glowing eyes fixed on the lattice. Presently a very white-faced man appeared just for a fleeting second, the face pressed up against the lattice and the eyes fixed on my wife whose face was in the light of the reading lamp.

Before anything else could happen, Pilot sprang from his crouching attitude on the floor, where the man could not have noticed him, and landed with a roar bang against the lattice, which bulged outwards with his weight and possibly struck the man's face, which was pressed against it. Even if his nerves were in first-class condition, that sudden lion-like roar would have terrified.

But word got around and as the years passed we realised we were the only house round about never pestered by beggars, never attempted by burglars – and burglary was a common problem round about.

We heard later from a man arrested for burglary at another house that word had got out in the criminal fraternity that they should by all means avoid any attempt on our house. Our dog had apparently become a legend in the underworld and tales of its strength and ferocity had been exaggerated to the point that many people thought we kept a lion not a domestic pet!

Lionel Fletcher, Skipper My Chum, 1935

Charity Training

F ROM THE DAWN of the railway era until well after the end of World War Two, dozens of mainline railway stations employed charity dogs. Originally kept as pets by stationmasters they were fitted with collecting boxes and wandered the platform hoping that kind passengers would drop a few coins into their boxes. Charitable organisations encouraged the idea of charity dogs because they were so much more effective than humans at extracting money from passers-by.

In a bizarre twist, many of these dogs became even more effective collectors after they had died because they were often sent to a taxidermist to be stuffed and put in a glass case on the platforms where they had once worked. A collection box was neatly built into the glass case.

Many dogs were the third or fourth generation to work as collection dogs and their names can still be found in histories of rail travel – there was Wimbledon Nell, Brighton Bob, Swindon Bruce and Rebel at Oldham.

One collecting dog spent eight years – while alive – at Waterloo and then a further eighty-three years at the same station after death and in that time must have collected thousands of pounds for charity.

Many of the collecting dogs learned tricks to help persuade passengers to pay up – they would shake hands or stand up on their hind legs; they were regularly presented with medals by the newspapers which reported frequently on their successes.

One or two dogs stole the money they were given to buy biscuits at the station café; others were occasionally set upon by thieves, turned upside down and shaken to extract their coins.

After British Rail was created at the end of the Second World War dull, boring officials decided that railway dogs did not fit the sleek modern businesslike image they hoped to portray and the charity dogs were quietly retired. The last working charity dog was Laddie, an Airedale Terrier who worked full time at Waterloo in London until 1956.

Sadly, many of the stuffed dogs in their beautiful mahogany and glass cases were simply thrown away by the idiots who took over the running of the railways.

Station Jim who worked his whole life at Slough was one of the last to go. In the 1970s he still looked out over the platform from his glass case until he too was consigned to history.

Martin Giles, Railway Memories, 1990

Cash Collector

A BLIND MAN named Frank Robinson, living near Sardis, Mississippi, used to have two smart little mutts that helped him make a success of his begging expeditions to nearby towns.

One of the dogs, on leash, led Frank safely down the street, and the other trotted along with a small bucket tied to his collar. 'Help the poor blind man,' Frank said as they walked along, and passers-by dropped coins into the bucket.

The little beggar carrying it was thorough, all right, for he didn't overlook anybody in working a street. He trotted into stores, offices and every other likely-looking place, and people, amused and touched by the cleverness and pathos of the stunt, responded generously.

Some tried to tease him by pretending they were going to take his money, but a warning growl told them that such a joke wasn't to be carried too far. Any hand that went too far into that bucket would get nipped.

'Yes, sir? He's onto his job, ain't he? – that l'il dog,' says Frank proudly. And well might he be proud, for the dog helps him earn a very fair living.

Eldon Roarke, *Just a Mutt*, 1947

Life Down Under

I THOUGHT perhaps your readers might care to hear about the best-known dog in Australia, and his curious mode of life. His name is Railway Bob, and he passes his whole existence on the train, his favourite seat being on the top of the coal box.

In this way he has travelled many thousands of miles, going over all the lines in South Australia. He is well known in Victoria, frequently seen in Sydney, and has been up as far as Brisbane!

The most curious part of his conduct is that he has no master, but every engine driver is his friend. At night he follows home his engine driver of the day, never leaving him, or letting him out of his sight until they are back in the railway station in the morning, when he starts off on another of his ceaseless journeyings. I have not seen him on our line for some time; but noticed with regret last time he was in the station that he was showing signs of age, and limping as he walked.

Adelaide Cresswell, *The Times*, 24 August 1895

Canine Nurse

JACK, A ROUGH-HAIRED fox-terrier of quiet disposition, but a good ratter, and an inveterate enemy to strange or neighbouring cats, of whom, to my sorrow, he has slain at least one, became without effort the attached friend of a minute kitten introduced into the house last November.

This friendship has been continued without intermission, and is reciprocated by the now full-grown cat. She, unfortunately, got caught in a rabbit-trap not long ago, but escaped with no further injury than a lacerated paw, which for some time caused her much pain and annoyance.

Every morning Jack was to be seen tenderly licking the paw of the interesting invalid, to which kind nursing no doubt her rapid recovery may be attributed; and though she is now more than convalescent and able to enjoy her usual game of play, he still greets her each morning with a gentle inquiring lick on the injured paw, just to see if it is all right; before proceeding to roll her over in their accustomed gambols.

This seems to me a marked instance of individual affection overcoming race-antipathy.

Blanche Rochfort, *The Spectator*, 18 May 1895

Bird Fancier

I THINK THE following history, to which I can bear personal testimony, may be found not uninteresting to your readers. At this delightful house in Perthshire, where I am on a visit, there is a well-bred pointer, named Fop, who, when not engaged in his professional pursuits on the moor, lives chiefly in a kennel placed in a loose-box adjoining the other stables attached to the house.

Nearly a year ago there were a pair of pigeons who lived in and about the stable yard. One of the birds died, and its bereaved mate at once attached itself for society and protection to the dog, and has been its constant companion ever since.

On the days when the sportsmen are not seeking grouse the dog is in his kennel, and the pigeon is always his close attendant. She roosts on a rack over the manger of the stable, and in the day-time is either strutting about preening her feathers, taking her meals from the dog's biscuit and water tin, or quite as often sitting in the kennel by his side, nestling close to him.

Fop, who is an amiable and rather sentimental being, takes no apparent notice of his companion, except that we observe him, in jumping into or out of his kennel while the pigeon is there, to take obvious care not to crush or disturb her in any way.

The only other symptom Fop shows is of being jealous for the pigeon's comfort and convenience. When two chickens from the stable-yard wandered into the apartment where the dog and pigeon reside, he very promptly bit their heads off as if in mute intimation that one bird is company, and two (or rather three) are none.

The story is rather one of a pigeon than a dog, for it is quite evident that she is the devoted friend, and that he acquiesces in the friendship. On the days when Fop is taken, to his infinite delight, on to the moor, the pigeon is much concerned.

She follows him as far as she dare, taking a series of short flights over his head, until a little wood is reached, through which the keeper and dogs have to take their way.

At this point her courage fails her, and she returns to the stable, to wait hopefully for her comrade's return. This singular alliance is a great joy and interest to the keepers, coachmen, and grooms of the establishment, and as the keeper gave me a strong hint that the story ought to be told in print, adding that he had seen much less noteworthy incidents of animal life promoted to such honour, I have ventured to commit the story to paper.

J. F., *The Times*, 22 September 1888

Not Worth His Salt

WHEN BOGEY first began to haunt the doctor, his family were still lamenting the loss of Presto, a white foxterrier greatly beloved by all on account of his many accomplishments.

No dog was ever so intelligent as Presto. There was nothing he could not do, from marching round the garden on his hind legs to fetching the doctor's evening paper from the railway station two miles away. It had been the custom of the house to give Presto a penny when he did anything specially clever, and he always took it to the nearest bakers, dropped it neatly on the counter with a knowing air, and waited for a bun in exchange.

He was not to be cheated, and knew perfectly well if the baker tried to give him a halfpenny bun instead.

Indeed, he let everyone know about it by barking furiously, and could only be quietened by giving him his fair exchange for the penny.

The doctor always declared that when Presto fetched the paper he would know perfectly well if he was given an early edition instead of the latest – but the newsboy, warm admirer though he was of the dog, refused to corroborate this.

It was, however, Presto's sporting instincts that led to his undoing. He simply could not keep away from the rabbit warren, and one day he pursued a fine old buck down its hole, and, alas, never came out again. The doctor missed him sadly and when his grandchildren appeared with a puppy which the boys had exchanged for a home-made aeroplane and a discarded football, he refused to allow it to cross the threshold, and though more than one of his patients offered him dogs, worthy successors to Presto, he shook his head with unmistakable finality.

No one was better loved in the little fishing village where he lived, and though the church on the hill was well attended, and the parson fairly popular, it was to 'th' ould doctor' that people went when they were in trouble. The gallant way in which he carried on in spite of his age was a source of pride to them. 'He'm seventy-odd if he'm a day,' they used to say as they watched his upright figure swinging up the hill, 'but thar i'nt a young 'un who kin touch 'im.'

His face was still smooth and pink as a boy's under its snowy thatch, but they thought he seemed to stoop a little after Presto's disappearance, and something of its cheery ring went out of his voice as he ordered White Star, his mare, to trot home.

White Star missed Presto almost as much as the master did, for he had always run at her heels – and even occasionally snapped at them on the way home, when he wished to hurry her because his supper was waiting. When, presently, a gaunt-looking stray, known by the village lads as 'Bogey,' took to following him on his rounds, the doctor was anything but gratified, but the dog stuck to him, and always ambled up for a kind word when he dismounted from White Star.

No one knew much about Bogey, except that he had been abandoned as a puppy on the village green. His sire had probably been as disreputable as himself, but his mother was a respectable Newfoundland.

From her he inherited remarkable swimming powers, and his clumsy body never appeared to such advantage as in the water. When he dived in at high tide from the parade wall, and breasted the waves like some big black seal, he was much admired. In those bad days, however, he was more likely to be bombarded by the village boys with sticks and stones, which he bore patiently, along with all the rude remarks about his personal appearance which daily echoed after him.

One day the doctor tossed him a casual biscuit, and thereafter Bogey would not leave his side. There was something touching in that devotion, and the doctor yielded to it at last, in spite of himself.

'Twenty times pelted, your dog will remember the morsel you gave him. Cherish your friend for an age, and he turns, for a trifle, at last!' he quoted from a wise old Persian sheikh who, centuries ago had so summed up dog and human nature.

One afternoon, when he spied the outcast waiting patiently in the sun-baked road outside his garden, he broke his fixed determination to take no notice of him and carried out a drink of water to what he now jokingly called his 'black shadow'.

That settled the matter as far as Bogey was concerned. He paused to lick the old man's hand before he slaked his thirst, and when he had lapped up the last drop he sat down by the surgery door as if he had a right to be there. Nothing and nobody could make him leave it, except to snatch his meals or follow the doctor and White Star.

He soon came to know all the regular patients by sight, and let them go past him with a wag of his tail, but anyone who was furtive or down-at-heel he sniffed at suspiciously, and they were only allowed to push open the green baize door after he had voiced his objections quite clearly by means of sniffs and growls.

By this time the doctor had become resigned to his adoption, and Bogey, feeling his way tactfully, ventured first into the hall, then into the nursery where the latest child of the doctor's favourite daughter crawled about in the sunshine on the faded carpet, amid the shabby collection of toys which had already been the delight of several past generations.

The baby found the big black dog a fine change from teddy bears and woolly balls, but his mother and the older children were not so pleased. 'He's a silly ole thing!' declared little Gladys, when she had wasted much time in trying to persuade him to sit up and beg, or to shut the door when he was told. 'You're not worth your salt, Bogey,' the doctor remarked one day in fun, when the dog had met his grandsons' command to 'die for your country' with nothing but puzzled grunts.

All the same, he patted the rough coat, and even invited him to lie by the study fire, which was always lit on chilly evenings. That was the dog's idea of bliss, and he sighed long and deeply in contentment. Bogey was a one-man dog, entirely devoted to the doctor, with the one exception of the baby, towards whom he displayed a pitying sort of regard.

If the study was closed to him, he occasionally visited the nursery, and it was on one of these visits that he justified his existence. Next door to the doctor lived a little old maid who kept a fierce Manx cat which she had not the heart to get rid of, though it was really very bad-tempered. One day the cat found its way into the nursery next door, where the baby was sitting alone on the floor. The child thought this promised some fun, and scrambled towards Pussy with outstretched hands, but the cat drew back and crouched, spitting and hissing, sheathing and unsheathing its sharp claws.

Downstairs, Bogey had just had the worst of an attempt to keep out of the surgery a ragged boy who came with a medicine bottle in his hand, and he was standing at the foot of the stairs still expressing indignation at his failure when he heard an unexpected sound from up above. His head went up, and in one bound he was up the stairs. He reached the child before its mother could, and saw the cat, already something of an enemy of his, with paw raised dangerously near the baby's face. On this occasion there was no gate-post for her to get behind, no tree for her to climb and escape him. Bogey leaped on her with a yelp of rage. The baby stopped crying. The cat flew out of the window, and Bogey went back to his self-elected duties below, with a gratifying sense of a job well done, while the child's mother stayed to see that no repetition of the incident occurred.

Kind treatment and good feeding made a new dog of Bogey, but he never quite lost the hunted look born of his early life. An impatient note in his master's voice was sufficient to make him cringe, and he was never at ease in the presence of boys, even the doctor's grandsons. They could be pleasant enough sometimes – when, for instance, they had pieces of gristle on their plates to get rid of, but as a general rule Bogey found it best to keep clear of them. Fortunately for him, the two grandsons decided he was too hopelessly dull for anything, and rarely bothered about him.

One curious trait in Bogey was that he became strangely disturbed whenever the storms blew up and the great waves came crashing in, curling over with crests of foam and breaking in thunder on the shore. On such wild nights he used to leave the safe shelter of the warm study and stay down by the sea until early morning. The coast-guards knew him well by sight, and had many a story of his 'queer ways' to tell the doctor when he strolled down by the sea after his work was over to watch the sunset.

Then Bogey's great delight was to swim out after the sticks he threw for him into the gleaming waters. No matter how far out they fell, Bogey always found them and brought them back, and was so proud of his accomplishment that it was often difficult to persuade him to come out of the water.

As time went on, the doctor grew fonder than ever of him. Bogey, and only Bogey, knew when he felt tired, and it was to the dog that he confided how he longed to stop work and to rest his old bones. The dog may not have been as accomplished as Presto, but his sympathy was warm and unfailing. Unspoken gratitude shone in his eyes and was more to his master's mind than the voluble thanks he sometimes received from his patients – from one Molly Dennison, for instance.

'All right, my good woman! Say less, and think more!' was often his unspoken reply to her as she stood at her cottage door when he passed through the village, and called down blessings on his head until he was out of ear-shot for ridding her of her rheumatism.

Old Molly was not a pet of his, for he had a shrewd suspicion that it was on her account that a sad little wife in a small brown cottage down by the cove was so often unhappy. The doctor had brought Nell Summers into the world eighteen years before, and when she married Molly Dennison's hot-tempered son, Dick, who had always been the apple of his mother's eye, and spoilt by her every day of his life, the doctor guessed pretty well how things would be.

'What's wrong to-day?' he asked her gently one bleak, grey morning, when he found her with her face stained with tears. She would not tell him for some time, though in the end he gathered that she and Dick had quarrelled, and that they had parted with bitter words.

'He wanted me to have his mother here while he was away,' she sobbed, 'an' I told him I would bide alone, come what might … Then he shouted at me, an' said I was unnateral, an' never thought of anyone but mysel'. An' I said he wur hard and thankless, an' that I never wanted to see his face agin.' 'Tut, tut!' cried the doctor, giving her a little shake. 'Dry your eyes and get things straight for him. He'll be back tonight, and won't want to find you sick with crying. You are like two silly children who quarrel for the sake of making it up again. You'll kiss and be friends directly he comes home.' 'The sea's so cruel!' sighed Nell. 'Listen to the wind? It was blowing all night long, an' I thought of the rocks, an' of Dick's ship. Oh, I wish I'd never said it! I must ha' been mad!'

The doctor soothed her as best he could, and called in at old Molly's on his way back to warn her to be gentle if she came across her. It was very rarely that he spoke in vain, and old Molly was anxious enough herself at the rising storm, so she made her way to the brown cottage with a peace-offering of honey from her one hive.

That was the night of 'th' Great Storm' along that coast which is still talked about by the fisherfolk. It raged from sunset until noon the following day, and it seemed as though all the furies had been let loose to ride the sea. Bogey stayed on the shore all night howling in chorus with the wind rushing to and fro in excitement as rockets went up from a ship in distress.

Again and again the men tried to launch the lifeboat; but it could not pass the boiling surf. Two of them were dragged down by the sucking current, and after that they stopped for a while.

When the first light of dawn showed in the sullen sky they saw a sinking wreck on the jagged rocks that fringed the bay, and tried again. But still in vain. The tide beat them back, and it seemed as though the end of those men, clinging to their shattered masts, was only a matter of minutes.

The doctor paced the beach, his face drawn with grief, for he knew them, every one. The sight of Bogey, who had stopped racing madly about and had come to stand beside him, gave him an idea. A forlorn hope, he thought, but, catching up a spar of wood, he called the dog, and threw it as far as he could in the direction of the wreck.

'To the ship! To the ship, dog!' he shouted, and Bogey dived through the surf swimming for dear life, as if he were a fish. The spar of wood had fallen a little short of the wreck, but young Dick Dennison, clinging to the rigging, recognized Bogey's strong black body, tossed on the crest of a wave. With the ready wit of men who take their lives in their hands each time they go to sea, he fastened one end of a long rope to another stick, and flung it towards him. Bogey dropped the stick he was carrying, and caught it instantly. At the same moment a huge, powerful wave, as though sent by some impulse of mercy, swept him back to the shore.

How he survived the drag of the surf was always a miracle to the fisherfolk, who believe to this day that some good spirit lent him strength and courage. Now lost to sight beneath the foaming waters, now tossed and shaken by the breakers as if he were floating driftwood, the dog held on to his piece of wood, on which depended the safety of eight otherwise doomed men.

It seemed to the onlookers hours rather than minutes before Bogey came within reach of their helping hands and, breathless and exhausted, was dragged on the beach. As he laid the stick at the doctor's feet a shout went up that even reached Dick's cottage, where the two women to whom he belonged clasped hands and prayed.

The rope was soon made fast, and, hand over hand, the men swarmed along it to safety. Dick came last, and as he was pulled by friendly hands to safety the ship disappeared under the waves. No one had time just then to think of Bogey – not even his master. When they did he was nowhere to be seen: he had made his way back to the study fire, and there, gazing quietly into the glowing embers, he rested and dried his coat. Some friends of the doctor tracked him down, but in response to all their cries of praise he only gave a languid wag of his tail. His manner said quite plainly that their excitement bored him, but when they had gone he dragged himself nearer the doctor and rested his head against the old man's knee with a sigh of contentment that went straight to his master's heart.

L. Gask, *Not Worth His Salt*, 1910

No Other Dog Will Do

ONE CASE in particular stands out above all the rest. In the whole course of my activities nothing in human and animal interest approaches it. I must refrain from mentioning names, but the story is just as good without them; better, because it could have happened anywhere else in the world.

Four years ago, over on the East Side, not a great way north of the Sixties, a boy ten or eleven, son of a rich man residing on Park Avenue, picked up on Lexington Avenue a crippled, half-starved mongrel pup; called him Mike.

Into the house he smuggled the outcast and hid it in his bed, to which snug quarters he brought food and drink for the newcomer.

He made a rough bandage for the dog's bruised leg, but failed to give the pup a bath.

The next morning a housemaid, entering the bedroom, found the pair curled up in slumber. Being something of a dog fancier herself, she advised the boy to make a place for his pal in some other part of the mansion instead of in the bed linen. The kid agreed to this, but on the third night Mike and master hunkered together.

They were inseparable until the housekeeper, distracted by the untidiness of the new roomer, complained to her mistress, who in turn took the matter up with the boy's father, a person who didn't care especially for dogs or any other household pets.

Pop, a man of decision, summoned the butler and told that worthy to open the front door, place the pup gently on the sidewalk and then return to his duties.

Now the butler, who was a human kind of a guy, tipped the boy off right away, and the boy, without a hat, bolted for the street crying for his pup as though he had gone mad.

He ran all over the neighbourhood in a childish frenzy calling the dog's name. But Mike had vanished. I don't want to make this story too long, but when that kid returned from his search he was in a state bordering on hysteria.

The only sound that came from his lips was something between a sob and the hiccoughs. A doctor who was called in ordered the boy put to bed and administered mild opiates. The patient developed a temperature and by morning was in a state of complete exhaustion, with spells of mild delirium, during which he continually called for his dog.

The father, now thoroughly frightened and blaming himself for the plight of his son, borrowed a dog from a neighbour and brought it to the boy's bedside. Nothing doing; the kid merely glanced at the substitute for the lost Mike and turned away.

After three days and nights of anguish and uncertainty the fever was conquered and the delirium dispelled. But the hurt look in the lad's eyes remained. At this juncture in the case the father got an inspiration. That's what it was; an inspiration: Mike must be found and brought back to his sick master. No substitutes would do. Mike or nothing. Advertisements were placed in the evening newspapers. The Society for the Prevention of Cruelty to Animals sent out notices to all its men to keep a sharp lookout for a crippled Scotch and fox terrier mongrel, and in addition a citywide search was prosecuted among dog dealers. Two days later a man picked Mike up in the park at Yorkville, near the East River.

Though dirty almost beyond recognition, no time was lost in hustling Mike to the Park Avenue residence. The butler, who answered the doorbell, recognising the significance of the occasion, requested that the dog be brought without delay upstairs to the sick room. On tiptoe the nurse entered and placed the dog on the foot of the bed, where the boy lay asleep.

I have always regretted that I was not an eyewitness to what happened in that chamber. The nurse afterward told me about it. The moment Mike's feet touched the counterpane he stiffened, cocked his ears, sniffed a moment and with a yelp that was almost human jumped for the pillow and began to nose the clothing away from the form defined beneath.

Opening his eyes, as though interrupted in a dream, the boy threw out his arms, encircled the mongrel in a smothering embrace and burst into a flood of ecstatic weeping broken by the oft-repeated word, 'Mike! Mike! Mike!'

A few days following their reunion, the Poor Little Rich Boy and Mike, washed for the occasion, were seen gambolling together on the green of Central Park.

Robert Davies, *The More I Admire Dogs*, 1936

Lost Child

TOM AND Toby were the doggy playmates of a small boy on an Australian farm, years ago, and his aunt gave me an outline of the following story just after the little fellow had been lost and found again.

He is now a man, and may smile at the names I have given to the dogs, but they will do as well as any other. I remember quite well – that one dog was black and the other black with tan markings and white fore-paws and chest, and that they were sheep dogs. They were the boy's guardians when he was a baby, and they taught him to walk when he reached that stage in his development, for he would take a handful of Tom's hair, and a fistful of Toby's hair just where he could reach it on their ribs, pull himself up on to his baby feet, and stand there with triumph written all over his face. Thus he first felt his own feet under him and gradually grew stronger.

The dogs seemed to know all about it, and except when away on the work of the farm, they were always within the baby's reach. His mother feared nothing for her boy when the dogs were by his side, for they would have killed any slithering snake that dared rear its ugly head near her child – any wandering horse or cow, and even the cocks and hens, were kept at a distance if the baby slept in the open as was often the case; thus he had little need of a human nurse as far as his protection was concerned.

When his baby feet were stronger under him, he took the first hesitating steps (when his little legs went bandy and then knock kneed as they wavered beneath him), supported on either side by the dogs.

They understood quite well, and waited patiently as he hesitated or when he grew tired. Often when his mother went looking for him at meal times she would find him outside under one of the trees, his little curly head pillowed on Toby's soft coat, the little chap fast asleep, with Tom lying at hand on guard against all intruders.

Neither dog would move until he woke, and no one except his mother was allowed to disturb his rest. Often the mother smiled and let him sleep on, knowing that when he awoke the dogs would bring him home, for they knew she was waiting for him. So it was that in the district stories were told by people who had seen the little lad toddling home between the two dogs, piloted to the chair where his Mother was waiting for him with his meal, and the three of them were spoken about far and wide.

The dogs became his playmates as he reached the stage for games and fun. They ran and brought back his ball, they pretended to dig for imaginary rabbits, accompanied by the peals of childish laughter as they threw the earth into the air behind them and redoubled their efforts when he urged them on. How he loved to see the earth on their noses when they looked up during the digging process, and how excited he was when one day they actually dug out a live rabbit which galloped off, pursued by the yelping dogs, who came back without him, for Mr Rabbit had found a refuge in a neighbour's burrow.

The boy reached three years of age, and life was a happy business for him on that big farm, with the open spaces, and the lovely dogs, and games and fun every day.

But he wanted to know what was in the great big world across the fields; he wanted to find out all by himself.

One day he persuaded the dogs to take him farther afield. They were having great fun, for they had found a regular town full of rabbits, and every time Tom and Toby dug a fresh hole, one, and sometimes two and three rabbits rushed out and ran away, sometimes the two dogs chased two rabbits in different directions, and he chased a third rabbit in another direction, the dogs barking, while he was shouting with excitement.

This was something like life! He was getting a really big boy now; he could look after himself, and was not going home while all this fun was going on. His progress led him into the bush, where some wild creature ran away from the dogs and seeing how delighted their young master was, they set off in pursuit, yelping and barking, while he toddled along in the rear shouting to them to catch it.

Time and place were alike forgotten, and the night came quickly and quietly and found him asleep with one dog for a pillow and the other cuddled up close to keep him warm. There was a great deal of work to do on the farm in those days so the women were busy with cooking and other necessary work, and no one missed the little fellow until the night drove the workers in from the fields for their supper.

The mother expected to see the men bringing him home, perhaps riding one of the big horses; the men expected to see him sitting in his high chair in the big kitchen waiting for his meal, at which he always said his baby grace. Questions were asked and answered, men ran out to whistle for the dogs, and holler long and loud, in the hope that at least one of the dogs would come running in to let them knew that the other dog and the boy were coming along.

The supper was forgotten in the excitement and anxiety; horses were saddled and a search-party went off, some to ride along the roads and tracks and some to walk across the fields where the boy generally played.

But midnight came; tired watchers faced still more tired searchers who had come back to report failure. Neighbours began to ride up, having heard the news. Without delay they formed fresh search parties, for they all knew the dread danger which surrounded a child lost in that dense bush. The mother tried not to think of the poisonous snakes crawling through the long grass or in and out of the thick bushes.

Her husband reminded her that the dogs would protect the child but he himself was shuddering as he thought of the great holes left by prospectors who had dug for gold all through that district in past days.

Some of the holes were very deep, and some were half full of water, and some were covered with a thin layer of rubbish through which a child might fall and be lost forever. The night found no one in bed. Even the women were out with lanterns; the men searched for miles until the day dawned, when they were forced to come back for feed and rest.

Fresh helpers arrived instantly until it seemed as if every man in that scattered district was searching for the little boy with the two dogs. Their one hope that he was still alive lay in the fact that neither of the dogs had come back.

Surely they would have come seeking aid if anything serious had happened? All through the day they searched, but the sun sank in the west, and midnight dragged round again, and still no sign.

Experienced bushmen shook their heads, and the mother felt she had no tears left to shed. Just as the second day began to dawn the mother heard scratching at the kitchen door, then the whining of a dog. She had not undressed since the boy had gone, and she reached the door before anyone else had heard a sound, and there was Tom, jumping and whining, and licking her hands, and running off towards the field and back again, as much as to say, 'You follow me.'

In less time than it takes to tell men were on their horses following the dog, which galloped on in front of them, yelping every now and again in his eagerness, but leading on all the time, through field after field and then into the deep bush, until they came to a place where the earth had sunken down in a hollow with very steep sides – there at the bottom of the hollow they found the little lad, fast asleep with his head pillowed on Toby's ribs.

At home the mother was getting hot milk and other things ready, and when his daddy came into the kitchen carrying the sleeping boy, and laid him in the arms of his mother, outstretched to take him, the man's arms went round the two of them, while a quiet thanksgiving went up to the unseen, loving Father.

They remembered that it was written: 'Surely goodness and mercy shall follow me all the days of my life.'

In a day or two the house was again filled with chatter, and then the whole story came out little by little. It was no wonder the mother put an arm around each dog when the little chap told her that each night they cuddled close to him and kept him warm.

He could not get out of the hollow into which he had slipped when chasing a rabbit. He had tried very hard, and both dogs had done their best to help him and he was not old and wise enough to have thought of sending one of the dogs home, until Tom himself at last set off on the journey while the lad was asleep, watched over by Toby.

Until the days when their work was ended, both dogs were loved and cared for at the farm, and they were still the boy's chums and constant companions till the time when he laid their old bodies to rest amidst the very soil in which they used to dig to out rabbits for his delight.

Lionel Fletcher, *Skipper My Chum*, 1935

Keeping Shop

MY FAVOURITE dog was a little Jack Russell that lived to be eighteen. She was called Rusty and had a strange habit of rushing at the door when a passer-by so much as paused outside the shop. But, strangely, she never barked. Instead she bumped the glass-panelled door continually with the side of her head and then, if the passer-by pushed the door and came into the shop, she threw herself continually at their shins as they crossed towards the counter. But all this was done in absolute silence.

Most of the shop regulars loved her, but especially the farm boys who were always asking me if I would let her have a litter or two. But the one time we tried to get a mate for her she bit her suitor on the rump and then leapt four feet into the air into my arms.

To stop her nudging the customers I installed a tall wooden stool behind the counter and here she sat for years staring hopefully at the door and jumping up and spinning round on the top of her seat when a customer came in.

And at the age of ten she finally started to bark. The first time it happened I had left the front of the shop to go into the storeroom behind. I heard a little high pitched bark and not believing my ears went along the corridor and back into the shop. Sure enough Rusty had barked because a customer had come in. I never had to install a bell on the door because from then on I left the shop in her charge whenever I fancied a cup of tea or a rest because she never failed to bark when someone came calling.

J. B. H. Smith, *Memories*, 1913

Dogs Before Nazis, 1938

THE BRITISH are famous, among other things, for tolerance – while Europe, from France to Poland and beyond, persecuted the Jews during the years leading up to and through the Second World War Britain provided a haven for Jewish refugees; in the 1970s when Idi Amin expelled every Asian from Uganda, Britain offered them a home and in recent years more migrants have targeted the UK precisely because of its reputation for tolerance.

But if the British love foreigners they love their dogs even more. Indeed the British love of dogs is considered one of our most delightful eccentricities – visitors to Britain over the past three hundred years have commented again and again on the fact that the average Briton is much fonder of his dog than of his friends and family. A long forgotten magazine once printed the results of a survey of its readers: the survey revealed that given the choice of sleeping with their wives or their dogs the majority (the figures worked out roughly three to one) would prefer the dog!

One dog that enjoyed the tolerant affection of the British belonged to Hitler's ambassador to Britain in the 1930s, Joachim Von Ribbentrop. In 1938 Ribbentrop's dog Giro died and as a gesture of goodwill he was allowed to bury it in the gardens to the left of the Duke of York's Column just off the Mall.

Despite the fact that when war came Von Ribbentrop immediately became a hate figure for the British no one would have dreamt of disturbing the grave of his dog – probably because they had always preferred the dog anyway. The dog's little headstone can still be seen today.

Ivor Brown, *London Memories*, 1947

Chapter Five

SUPER CLEVER

Long Distance Laurie

A SCOTTISH terrier owned by the late Mr Appleby, a widower of Glasgow, affords an instance of the almost unbelievable intelligence of dogs.

Mr Appleby, a solicitor by profession had long lived in Arundel in Sussex. He enjoyed a flourishing business there and was widely respected by his clients. He specialised in the law regarding the buying and selling of land and was famous for his wry jokes and about farmers being unhappy whether they were buying or selling, leasing or repairing, eating or drinking, awake or asleep. Despite his jests he was the man the farmers turned to most often when they were in any sort of difficulty, whether in regard to sales and rental agreements, disputes over boundaries or the sale of corn or other merchandise.

An old farmer who hated to pay for anything offered a lower fee than had been initially agreed to his solicitor following the satisfactory sale of a parcel of land.

My Appleby knew what a mean old devil the farmer was and made a face which was as much as to say, 'I will hold you to our agreement'.

The farmer hummed and hawed, pled poverty and finally offered payment part in cash and part in the form of a dog.

Mr Appleby again looked unconvinced but agreed to at least lay eyes on the offered animal.

He had not previously kept a dog and had no real intention of agreeing to take this or any other mutt instead of agreed cash but something about the little dog changed his mind and he agreed to this novel form of payment, much to the delight of the farmer.

The dog, which he decided to call Laurie, quickly became Appleby's pride and joy – and his best friend. They travelled all over the country together and when Mr Appleby went to church the dog would accompany him in the trap sitting up and looking out intelligently over the surrounding fields. He never barked but when he wanted attention would instead run to his master, sit alertly in front of him and then slowly raise his right paw in the air and begin waving it until Mr Appleby picked him up or followed him out the door.

On his retirement Mr Appleby returned to Glasgow

where he bought a large and comfortable house and installed his dog and his old housekeeper.

The three lived happily there for a number of years until one summer Mr Appleby decided to re-visit his old haunts in the South Country.

He and Laurie set off by train and the little dog clearly loved the journey insisting on sitting on its master's lap all through the journey except when he visited the dining car.

They stayed at a grand hotel in Arundel, Laurie sleeping every night on Mr Appleby's bed and joining him each morning for breakfast in the dining room where he delighted the other diners with his gentle intelligent ways and quiet nature.

Two weeks they spent visiting old friends, walking the old familiar farm tracks, the woods and streams. On the morning on which they were due to return to Scotland, Appleby woke and found Laurie gone. He searched through the hotel and made enquiries there and at the local police station. No one had seen the little dog. Appleby put off his return for a day and then two days. Still no sign of the dog and no news of his whereabouts.

On the fourth day and with a heavy heart Appleby decided that poor Laurie must have met with a terrible accident. He packed his things and returned to Glasgow. A month later to the day he heard a scrabbling at his front door and on opening it discovered Laurie furiously wagging his tail but terribly thin and with patches of fur missing here and there. Indeed he was so emaciated that he might easily be mistaken for another dog. Mr Appleby took him in and nursed him. Within a week he was his old self again but the mystery of how he travelled hundreds of miles back to Glasgow from Sussex was never solved.

Glasgow Herald, June 1840

Uncanny Canine

IN RECENT years, a system of National Sheepdog Trials has been inaugurated in England, Scotland and Wales. At these meetings all but the very best dogs are eliminated, and teams of twelve are selected to represent the respective countries at an International Trial, which is usually staged early in September.

This Trial lasts three days, and for competitors and spectators alike, they are days packed with thrills and excitement. From all over the kingdom, weather-beaten shepherd kings and their faithful four-footed allies gather to compete for the Championship title.

The International is held at a different centre every year, and nobody who has the opportunity should miss seeing it. The sagacity of these sheepdogs is truly amazing. It has been claimed of some dogs that they can identify one of their own sheep among a flock of hundreds of others, that they will pick out and separate from the flock designated sheep; and even that they can count, and know when one of the flock has strayed.

A well-authenticated story substantiating the last claim relates to a collie named Shep, owned by a certain Mr David Pierce, of Heosho, Missouri. Shep's daily task was to care for the flock of about one hundred sheep owned by Mr Pierce.

Every morning the dog drove the sheep from the corral along a lane for half a mile to the woods, where he kept them until about four o'clock in the afternoon, when he would round them up and start them home. When they reached the mouth of the lane, Shep would make his way through the flock, and going to the corral gate, would bark and wait for someone to come and open it. Then he would take his stand just inside the gate, and as the sheep passed into the corral he made sure that they were all there.

Two Kansas men were in Mr Pierce's neighbourhood one day, buying sheep. Hearing about this dog they went to Mr Pierce, to try the animal, and to buy him, if he were able to 'make good'. Mr Pierce decided to show them what the dog could really do.

'This is just about the hour for Shep to bring the sheep home,' said Mr Pierce, 'and the best test is the dog himself. When Shep leaves the sheep and comes to the gate for someone to open it, you catch one of the sheep near the mouth of the lane, take it down in the woods, and hide it, and we will see what Shep will do. I really don't know because I have never tested him in this way before.'

The sheep was caught and tied in the woods, and the gate was kept closed until the Kansas men got back. Then it was opened; Shep took his stand inside as usual, and the sheep went into the corral.

But no sooner had the last sheep passed into the enclosure, then Shep gave unmistakable signs that something was wrong. He sprang into the lane, looked in every direction, ran back into the corral, and looked the flock over more carefully; then out into the lane again, and down towards the woods he ran as fast as his anxious feet could carry him. Finding the trail of the men, he tracked them to the lost sheep.

Two hundred dollars was offered by the Kansas men for Shep, but Mr Pierce informed them that he would almost as soon part with one of his children.

Our Dumb Animals, 1930

Homing Terrier

A LARGE, handsome Scotch terrier, a few years ago, living then at Guildford, in Surrey, evidently understood a large part of the conversation he overheard. Though apparently not noticing the speakers before, and certainly not addressed by them, he no sooner heard the word 'robber' or 'thieves,' than he growled loudly his threatened vengeance.

When the housemaid was going to remain upstairs for an hour or two, and not likely to hear the doorbell, she used to say, 'Pincher, bark when the bell rings'.

As soon as this charge was given, Pincher would leave, even in winter, his warm place on the dining room rug, place himself on the mat at the foot of the stairs in the hall, and whenever the doorbell rang, he would bark until the servant came down and attended to the applicant. He never barked when the bell rang at any other time.

Pincher never forgot old friends; and though greatly attached to his master at Guildford, he paid weekly visits to another part of the family living at Godalming, some miles distant, where he was brought up; going thither regularly on his own and when the fancy took him, and punctually returning home each evening.

After about a year, however, his master removed to London, and Pincher accompanied the family to their new abode at Pentonville in the northern suburbs of the city.

One day, soon after their arrival in town Pincher was missing. Evening came and night; but though he was watched for anxiously, the faithful creature was not seen. The next day passed in like manner; but soon fear and sorrow took the place of solicitude, for the thought arose that he might have been stolen, or perhaps, killed.

But, on the third day, Pincher appeared, weary, foot-sore, all over dirt, and, too much exhausted to utter a sound, he dropped at his master's feet. It was some time before he could be revived sufficiently to eat some food, though of this he was manifestly greatly in need.

The cause of this extreme exhaustion was then suspected, and his master, on writing to make inquiry, found Pincher had been to Godalming to see his old friends.

How he had found his way thither – for he had been brought to London by train – or how many miles he had gone out of the direct route, no one could tell. And, strange to tell, Pincher continued to take this long and arduous journey – thirty miles and more each way – at regular if infrequent intervals, until at length he seemed to find it too much for his strength, and so honour to his affection and sagacity – gave up the task.

Some years after, his master left the country, and gave Pincher as a parting gift to a friend.

Two years later Pincher's old master was again in London, and while driving through its streets, he saw a dog suddenly rush across the road, reach his carriage, and showing great excitement and delight, strive earnestly to get in. It was Pincher – poor Pincher – who, walking quietly along the road, thinking only of what he was about, suddenly caught sight again of the much-loved face of his former master and friend and could do nothing till he had caressed him in his ecstasy.

British Chronicle, March 1816

Sagacious Skipper

Jon laughed at me when I told him the story of how Skipper had left me in the lurch in the heat of the day. Of course he had warned me about using him while he was young, but now he was reassuring and prophesied that Skipper would develop into one of the best sheep-dogs in the country.

And his prophecy proved correct, for he became as faithful and dependable as Lassie, and as clever as Dubbo, who was certainly the best dog in the district. Skipper became a lamb specialist. With the small, active, timid merino sheep, a dog must be very fast, but with merino lambs of a few days or a few weeks old many good sheep-dogs are absolutely helpless.

At first the lambs will follow a horse, a man, or a dog, apparently quite unable to distinguish between any moving creature and their mothers. Then as they become strong on their legs and are being driven with a mob, they will sometimes rush off at full speed, and will not respond to the presence of a dog as the older sheep will.

They may jump over his back, or race shoulder to shoulder with him refusing to turn towards the place where the sheep are being driven. Sometimes in their nervousness they will leap over a precipice or into a creek or river, and therefore to prevent such a catastrophe a good lamb-dog is invaluable, as it takes great patience and skill on the part of a dog to manage them.

At times they may become worn out with rushing about, and lie exhausted on the ground, and it is extremely ludicrous to see a dog standing with head on one side looking at the lamb lying there, wondering what he can do now to persuade this irritating creature to get on its legs and join the flock. Skipper loved lambs, and they seemed to love and trust him. If a group of them rushed off in haste, he could easily out-distance them, and running around in front, many yards ahead of them, he would instantly lie down with the jolliest look imaginable on his face.

His brown eyes danced with anticipation and merriment, and his long tongue hung out of the side of his mouth, giving him a droll look. The lambs either halted or swerved as they saw that waiting figure.

If they halted, Skipper lay quietly watching and waiting for them to calm down. He never barked as he worked, unless he was told to 'speak up,' and with lambs he used his voice only at very critical moments, and his knowledge as to when to use it came from an instinct which no human being could explain. If they did not stop, but swerved, then he was off and again they found him lying in front of them with the same jolly look, as if saying: 'Well here I am, my dears, you see you cannot get away from me.'

Thus by degrees he would get them back to their bleating mothers. If one wild lamb rushed off by itself, he raced along by its side, with his shoulder pressing insistently against its body, and thus would bring it back in a circle to the place from which it had galloped. A tired lamb lying down in the bush or amongst the long grass, which might be lost sight of and left for the cruel carrion-crows to kill or blind, was Skipper's special care.

He would affectionately push it with his nose, endeavouring to get it to rise and move, and this he was very often successful in doing. Then he would steadily keep the lamb walking, nosing it along very gently, until it reached the waiting flock, or met its mother who had left the others to run and meet the lost one.

If he failed to induce the lamb to rise, he would put his nose under the soft little body and lift it to its feet, and then push it with an insinuating, coaxing movement of his head, all the time smiling with those gentle brown eyes, as much as to say: 'Come on, little one – have another try.'

I often sat on my horse for long periods just to watch, and to wonder.

Who taught him these things? No human being, certainly. I knew that his father, Dubbo, was wonderful with lambs, but this was something beyond Dubbo's skill. Often it would end by the lamb being transferred to a position in front of me on the horse, and thus it would be carried home or to a place of safety. Then Skipper's big tail would wag in a gesture of deep satisfaction, and he would get on with the work of keeping the mob of sheep moving.

One day, as I was driving some ewes and lambs, Skipper suddenly disappeared. I guessed he was after a stray lamb, but when he was absent for quite a long time I whistled long and loudly. Then his sharp ears appeared for a fleeting moment through the undergrowth, and he flashed me a signal, gave a staccato bark, and disappeared again. I was impatient and whistled a peremptory command, but he did not come back, so I went after him and saw his tail waving through the trees ahead of me.

I whistled again; he looked round at me, and laid his ears back in an affectionate way, waved his tail, but still kept moving away from me. So I gave chase, and that seemed to please him, for he set off faster than my horse could travel, looking over his shoulder every now and again to see that I was following. Then he disappeared, and I realized that he had gone down into the bed of a deep, dry creek which ran through that paddock. I rode along to the edge of the creek, which was about twenty feet deep, and there I saw a little lamb lying helpless on a ledge about eight or nine feet from the bottom. It had evidently slipped over the side, but a bush had broken its fall and kept it from continuing its descent to the bottom of the creek.

Skipper was soon alongside, gently pushing it, then putting his nose underneath its body and lifting it to its feet, but each time the poor creature just crumpled up and fell in a heap. I guessed it had been injured and was too weak to stand. I was wondering what to do, for it was well out of my reach, when, to my amazement, after Skipper had uttered a short bark, I saw him gently take the slack skin on the back of the lamb in his teeth. He lifted his head with the lamb hanging from his mouth, and wagging his tail, set about the difficult climb and finally laid the little thing at my feet, as a retriever or spaniel might have done with a duck or animal that its master had shot.

He looked up into my face, wagged his tail, and whimpered as much as to say: 'Now pick it up and carry it on your horse.' He had never done such a thing before, and I never knew him do it again.

Lionel Fletcher, *Skipper My Chum*, 1935

Shot in the Jaw

Philadelphia seems to have more than its share of brave dogs – or else Philadelphians are just more diligent about seeing that their canine heroes get the recognition due them.

In November, 1940 a bronze medal was awarded to Minnie, a five-year-old German Shepherd, for saving the life of her master, Morris Green, druggist, by continuing to fight armed bandits after they had shot her in the jaw.

The two bandits entered Mr Green's store, on the corner of Twentieth and Jefferson Streets, shortly before midnight. One of them pulled a pistol and quietly ordered Mr Green to go behind his prescription counter. It was a holdup.

At sight of the gun, Minnie, who had been stretched out on the floor watching the door, sprang to her feet. She looked anxiously at her master, uncertain whether he was dealing with friends or foes. When no command to attack came from him, she relaxed. Then the bandit with the gun made a tactical blunder.

Impatient because Mr Green wasn't moving fast enough to suit him, he reached out and gave him a shove with his free hand. In a flash Minnie's uncertainty was gone. She sprang upon the bandit and sank her sharp teeth into his pistol hand.

With a mighty effort he tore his hand out of her mouth, stepped back and fired. The bullet broke her jawbone. The bandits then turned and fled, with Minnie staggering after them. At the door the gunman whirled and pointed his pistol at Mr Green.

Once more Minnie sprang upon him, and once more she caught his hand. Her jaws were weak and bloody, but she held on with all her waning strength. The gun fired, but the bullet went wild. Out into the night the bandits ran, and Minnie collapsed. The brave dog was taken to the Veterinary Hospital of the University of Pennsylvania where she recovered, and several months later received her award.

Eldon Roarke, Just a Mutt, 1947

Life Saver

Pooch, a friendly little mutt of the fox-terrier class, was a dog with presence of mind. She was owned by Edwin Gross of Philadelphia and was awarded a bronze medal for saving the life of Mrs Beatrice Landis.

The story started with the sudden desire of Mrs Landis to take a ride on a sled. It was late in the evening when that sudden desire led Mrs Landis to take off on a mile long hill which extended from the front of her home. Alone and with the thrill of speed accentuating her enjoyment, the start was made.

About half-way down the hill there was a sharp turn which, due to a sudden drop in temperature, was covered with ice. By the time the sled and its lone occupant reached the turn, such a terrible speed had been attained that Mrs Landis was unable to steer and the sled crashed into a tree growing on the bank. One moment of splintering crash. Then unconsciousness.

Shortly after the Gross family was startled by the frenzied barking of Pooch at the front door. That was most unusual conduct for her, and Mr Gross jumped up and opened the door to see what it was all about.

But Pooch didn't dash into the room in fright. She dashed the other way, toward the road, still barking. Mr Gross and another member of the family followed, wondering. Up the road about a hundred feet they found Mrs Landis lying in the snow, apparently frozen. They placed her on the broken sled and dragged it to the house, and administered first aid. Much to their relief, they discovered she was still alive. In a few minutes she regained consciousness, although she was a badly injured woman.

They took Mrs Landis to her home and called a doctor. He found her suffering from exposure, concussion and contusions, and also found that she had several fractured vertebrae. She was sent to the hospital and placed in a cast. Another half hour of exposure would have been fatal to her. Pooch was a little heroine for thinking quickly and sounding the alarm.

National Review, Autumn 1931

Spanish Poodle

I HAD BOUGHT a Spanish poodle pup off an Irishman who assured me, 'Indade, sir, an' the dog knows all my childer do, only he can't talk.'

He shut doors, opened those with thumb-latches, and rushed upstairs and waked his mistress at words of command. One day we were starting to drive to our former home in the city, six miles distant, but the dog was refused his usual place in the carriage, and shut up in the house.

When we arrived, to our astonishment we found him waiting for us on the doorstep! We could not conceive how he got there, but upon inquiry found that he had got out, gone to the station, in some way entered the train, hid under a seat, and on arrival in the city threaded his way a mile through the streets, and was found quietly awaiting our arrival.

Letter to *The Times*, March 1894

Doll's House

THE HON. Grantley Berkeley states that Cranford House, the seat of his family in his early days, was as isolated and lonely a place as it is possible to conceive; and that it was his father's practice to drive down from London with four long-tailed black horses, that took two hours to get over the twelve miles, on a Saturday night, and to remain at Cranford till Monday morning. On one of these occasions Lord Berkeley was accompanied by his sister, Lady Granard, and they arrived at Cranford on the afternoon of Saturday, bringing with them no additional servants, but trusting simply to the maids in charge of the house.

Lord Berkeley's favourite pointer, Doll, accompanied them in the carriage; and as she was a stranger to the servants at Cranford, she attached herself to her master.

After enjoying the quietude of the place, and rambling about the gardens, all retired for the night, Doll lying, as was her invariable custom, on her master's bed. Slumber had continued undisturbed for some time, when, on partially opening his eyes, Lord Berkeley thought he heard some very slight bustle outside his door.

On listening, the fact became more certain; for he distinctly heard the slow and cautious sliding of a hand on the panels, as if feeling for the handle of the lock, and then the hand – for such it seemed to be – struck on the lock, and paused there as if in cautious suspense.

The pistols he always travelled with were lying loaded on a chair by his bed; so, reaching out his hand, he seized one, and waited for what was to follow. He had no light in the room, which was dark as pitch. Lord Berkeley could now hear the handle of the door turn, then the door slowly rub over the carpet, as it opened to admit the intruder.

Light as the step was, he nevertheless was next aware of its stealing towards his bed. At that moment, remembering that Doll was the best and most watchful house dog possible, and wondering at her silence, he stretched out his left hand, the right holding the pistol pointed at the advancing object, to feel if she were awake. Awake she was, and conscious, too, of the presence of the suspicious visitor; for her head was erect, her ears up, and her attention riveted.

This puzzled her master, for he knew that she would have flown at any stranger. Suddenly, while his hand was on her head, thump, thump, thump, went Doll's tail on the bedclothes, and her ears subsided into their recumbent position.

There was no one in the house except Lord Berkeley and his sister, that Doll knew; so, at once replacing the pistol on the chair, but with his strong right hand – and it was a very powerful one ready for any required action, he sat up in bed and awaited the result. The almost noiseless step came on, till the slight rustle that accompanied it proclaimed the object to be within reach. And now the mystery was solved, but in indescribable alarm: Lord Berkeley stretched out his hand, and in his grasp he seized Lady Granard's arm; she had been walking in her sleep and with a shriek now awoke to consciousness; and it was clear that but for Doll, Lord Berkeley's knowledge of the dog's fidelity, and his own cool presence of mind, he would have killed his sister.

Charles Williams, *Anecdotes of Dogs*, 1870

Going Shopping

DURING THE meeting of the British Association at Glasgow, a friend of mine had occasion to go one day from that place to Greenock on business. Hearing, on his arrival, that the person he wished to see was out, but expected shortly to return home, he determined to take a stroll about the town, to which he was a stranger. In the course of his walk he turned into a baker's shop and bought a bun. As he stood at the door of the shop eating his bun, a large dog came up to him and begged for a share, which he got, and seemed to enjoy, coming back for piece after piece.

'Does the dog belong to you?' my friend asked of the shop woman. 'No,' she answered, 'but he spends most of his time here, and begs halfpennies from the people who pass.'

'Halfpennies! What good can they be to him?'

'Oh, he knows very well what to do with them; he comes into the shop and buys cakes.'

This seemed rather a remarkable instance of cleverness even for the cleverest of animals, so, by way of testing its reality, my friend went out of the shop into the street, where he was immediately accosted by the dog, who begged for something with all the eloquence of which a dog is capable.

He offered him a halfpenny, and was rather surprised to see him accept it readily, and walk, with the air of a regular customer, into the shop, where he put his forepaws on the counter, and held out the halfpenny towards the attendant.

The young woman produced a bun, but that did not suit the dog, and he held his money fast.

'Ah,' she said, 'I know what he wants,' and took down from a shelf a plate of shortbread. This was right; the dog paid his halfpenny, took his shortbread, and ate it with decorous satisfaction. When he had quite finished he left the shop, and my friend, much amused, followed him, and when he again begged found another halfpenny for him, and saw the whole process gone through a second time.

This dog clearly had learned by some means the use of money, and not merely the fact of handing over coins. He clearly knew the value of different coins.

If he gave one penny he expected one scone; if he gave two he expected two and would bark if anyone tried to give him less than he had paid for.

Lawson Tait, *The Spectator*, 10 February 1877

Thinking about the Doctor

A QUEER THING occurred just now. Father was in the office, and heard a dog yelping outside the door; he paid no attention until a second and louder yelp was heard, when he opened it, and found a little brown dog standing on the step upon three legs. He brought him in, and on examining the fourth leg, found a pin sticking in it. He drew out the pin, and the dog ran away again. The office of my father, Dr Atlee, is not directly on the street, but stands back, having in front of it some six feet of stone wall with a gate. I will add, that it has not been possible to discover anything more about this dog.

This story reminds me of something similar that occurred to me while studying medicine in this same office nearly thirty years ago. A man, named Cosgrove, the keeper of a low tavern near the railroad station, had his arm broken, and came many times to the office to have the dressings arranged. He was always accompanied by a large, most ferocious-looking bulldog, that watched me most attentively, and most unpleasantly to me, while bandaging his master's arm.

A few weeks after Cosgrove's case was discharged, I heard a noise at the office door, as if some animal was pawing it, and on opening it, saw there this huge bulldog, accompanied by another dog that held up one of its front legs, evidently broken.

They entered the office. I cut several pieces of wood, and fastened them firmly to the leg with adhesive plaster, after straightening the limb. They left immediately. The dog that came with Cosgrove's dog I never saw before nor since.

Do not these stories adequately show that the dogs reasoned and drew new inferences from a new experience?

The Spectator, 26 June 1875

Sheepdog Genius

UP BLAIR ATHOLL way into Kinloch Rannoch country, which is about the centre of Scotland, I made inquiries concerning the black and white collie. 'Come wi' me,' said a shepherd to whom I went for information, 'an' I will gi' ye a somple o' sheep dog intelligence wi'out worruds.'

I followed him through heather and gorse until we reached an open meadow which broke upon a stretch of upland moor over a small plateau against the skyline. He stopped at the edge of the open field and whistled sharply two long, shrill notes. From a cottage half hidden in a nearby grove a black collie with a fringe of white around the neck and shoulders came bounding across the turf.

Twenty yards from his master the dog stopped and came to attention, his eyes questioning the shepherd. On the slope of the hill grazed a flock of black-faced sheep scattered in pairs, trios and larger groups, occupying perhaps fifty acres.

I was requested to select, anywhere within a radius of five hundred yards, three sheep grazing together. I selected a trio that were browsing among some grey granite rocks. At a casual glance they might easily have been mistaken for part of the landscape.

Without uttering a spoken word, the shepherd, resorting entirely to gestures, sent the collie up the hill through a dozen other groups of grazing sheep and had the selected three brought down on the meadow within twenty feet of where we stood.

During the operation the collie frequently turned to his master for instruction, but made no mistakes. Not another sheep on the hillside was in the least disturbed.

While I was still marvelling at the dog's wonderful exhibition, the shepherd motioned him to take the sheep back to the plateau. 'We ha' ane dog to tak' the sheep out and ane to bring them hame,' said he, 'but, mon, ye wouldna' be deesappointed to ken a collie thot can do both.' He then sent the dog with the three sheep back to the exact spot where he got them.

As a further test of the dog's intelligence, the shepherd had him cut out a single sheep – of my selection – which he drove down to the cottage. There the collie opened the gate to a small corral, worked the sheep in and closed the gate after it.

Not once during the whole test did the shepherd speak to the dog, nor did the sheep appear to have any opposition to the collie urging it along to a definite end.

There is something positively uncanny about the relationship between a shepherd and his dog; a harmony of thought that seems to be automatic, the dog never escaping from the control of the shepherd's intent.

A collie in action possesses all the appeal of a human being awaiting instruction from a superior intelligence; and the response is instantaneous. A well-trained sheep dog can interpret the signs of his master at a distance of two miles.

It is not unusual for a shepherd to send his dog out on the hills to bring in sheep that are picked up with a field glass. But this particular dog seemed to be able to reach sheep beyond the shepherd's ken. He told the dog to bring six sheep from the other side of the fell out of sight – the dog returned with six and then from elsewhere out of sight, five.

How could it have known the word six or five? Yet it did.

Robert Davies, *The More I Admire Dogs*, 1936

Guitar Player

I HAVE SEEN a few musical dogs, but all of them, with one exception, were vocalists. The only dog instrumentalist I have ever met was Carburettor. He twangs a mean guitar. Carburettor, a big, black, short-haired mongrel, belongs to Clarence Brown, a blind man of Natchez, Mississippi. He and Clarence tour around, putting on little shows on street corners and in parks, usually teamed up with a couple of other minstrels.

Clarence is a good showman, so he holds back Carburettor's number as a grand finale, given only for a special consideration.

He and his two assistants play a few guitar and tambourine numbers, do some deep-river singing and a bit of spirited tap dancing and pass the cup. Then Clarence tells them about the extra-special attraction, 'a wonderful thing they jest won't believe 'less'n they see it for their-selves – a dog that plays the gee-tar. Yas, suh! That dog settin' right there at his feet can sho pick that old gee-tar to a fare-you-well. But he can't do it 'less'n they drop forty cents in the cup.'

If it's a pretty large crowd, he makes it seventy-five cents. When the amount has been raised, Clarence tells Carburettor to raise up there and put his foot on the strings and they dive right into 'the little brown jug'. That's Carburettor's favourite.

As Clarence says, 'Old Carburettor, he really goes to town with that little brown jug.' Clarence sings, beats time on the guitar box with his right hand, and fingers the neck with his left. Carburettor picks the strings, some-times using one paw and sometimes two.

And you actually recognize the tune! Clarence and Carburettor even had a part in a movie! It came about this way.

They always play at the famous Natchez Pilgrimages. They play at Pilgrimage headquarters, and they also add to the deep South atmosphere at some of the beautiful and dreamy *ante bellum* mansions open to the public on those special occasions.

A movie executive who attended one of the Pilgrim-ages spotted them, and promised to use them in a movie some day. And eventually he kept his word.

Clarence and Carburettor spent twenty-one days at

Charlottesville, Virginia, where the picture was filmed. They got fifteen dollars a day and all expenses, and had a wonderful time.

Clarence says Carburettor is a mixture of German water spaniel and chow. He doesn't look anything like a chow except that he has a blue tongue.

'A white lady in Choctaw County give him to me when he was just a little puppy,' Clarence says. 'I had been wanting to get me a dog to lead me around. So when the lady give me the puppy, I said I wanted to make a wonderful dog outa him, and I said I wanted to give him a name no other dog would have. Then Carburettor jest popped into my mind.'

Clarence had heard about the blind man who had trained his dog to carry a little bucket and beg, and he decided that would be a good stunt to teach Carburettor.

'But that didn't seem to be amusement enough for folks,' he says. 'Besides, they had already done seen the other man's dog do that, so I figured I had to think up sump'n better.'

One day at the railroad station at Winona, Mississippi, J. Whiteman said to Clarence: 'That dog of yours looks pretty smart. He looks smarter than most dogs. Can he do things?'

'Oh, yas, suh' Clarence replied. And then an idea popped into his mind, just like Carburettor's name had.

'This dog here, he can play the gee-tar.'

'Lemme see him,' the man shot back. And Clarence was on the spot.

'Set down here in front of me, Carburettor,' he commanded. 'Come on here now. Put your paw up and play this here gee-tar.' Clarence started playing and singing and slapping at Carburettor playful-like, and Carburettor started pawing back and hitting the strings. Clarence was flabbergasted – but he knew he had found the stunt he was hunting. He had sump'n that would amuse the crowd more'n a dog passing a cup.

'That was a Tuesday,' he says, 'and by Sat'day I had him trained to pick the gee-tar.'

Eldon Roarke, *Just a Mutt*, 1947

Super Clever

FOR MORE than ten years till failing health prevented her, my best loved terrier Lucy collected my newspaper every morning from the village shop. She would scratch at the door at precisely the same time and set off at a run as soon as I opened the door.

What made this all the more remarkable was that the village shop was more than two-miles away.

At first she took the road and the carter would see her often and wave to her. Then the ploughman saw her cutting vigorously across the fields to shorten the journey.

Imagine my astonishment when the old shopkeeper and newsagent died and I changed my order and patronised a newsagent in a village in another direction entirely.

I had only to show Lucy once where the new shop was – we travelled there together in the gig – and next morning she set off and returned half an hour later with my paper. What was perhaps even more remarkable was that the paper suffered little damage from her mouth and one day the farm boy told me that he saw her sheltering under a tree during a shower. Was that a deliberate move to keep my paper dry?

The Times, 1902

Police Special

Many are the tales told of the intelligence of German police dogs. Numerous books on the breeding, the training and the history of these remarkable animals have been written. Some of the yarns told of these hunters of men are bombastic and incredible. With the idea of turning up one authentic case in which a police dog displayed actual reasoning power I called upon Director George Gazlow, head of the dog department of the Berlin police, and put the question.

Like all Germans in official life, Gazlow took ample time in which to reply. 'Reasoning power, even among human animals, is rare,' he replied finally. 'Why should one expect a dog to go beyond the limits of his instincts? Our dogs are trained to follow a scent, to proceed upon an established trail until the pursued person is caught up with, at which point the police take the case in hand.

'If there is any necessity for action, or a display of resistance, a police dog, guided always by his master, will fight to the death. He is trained to take orders from but one man and is friend or enemy in accord with the attitude of that one man.

'Not being called upon to take the initiative, or to proceed beyond the limits of his training and his instincts, why should one expect reasoning power in a police dog?'

'Then you know not of a single case,' I repeated. After another period of reflection he said

'Ach. Perhaps – possibly,' said he.

'That might be true of the great Frack. Come with me, we shall ask the trainers. Let them decide. This way – to the ground floor.'

Proceeding down a series of endless corridors Director Gazlow, letting himself into a dimly lighted room heavy with animal heat, beckoned me to enter. Six men dressed in civilian attire stood at attention. Six police dogs with blazing eyes came to static positions behind their masters and sniffed audibly. I seemed to be the object of their glittering inspection, based no doubt upon resentment that I had been captured and brought in without their assistance.

Director Gazlow uttered a sentence in German, evidently an endorsement of the stranger. Instantly every dog in the room registered 'welcome,' the nearest suffering my alien hand to rest upon his cold nose.

The chief of the dog department addressed a question to the trainers, receiving from all six of them in reply, after due deliberation, the word 'Frack'.

'I asked them,' said he, turning, 'which in their opinion was the most intelligent police dog we have ever had in our service. You heard them name Frack. I will now tell you the story of Frack's greatest performance, from which you may decide for yourself whether or no he had the power to reason.'

The director asked one of the trainers to hand him a framed chart that hung upon the wall; a chart that defined a landscape intersected by highways, fences and a railroad line, divided into fields with hedges, trees and gardens.

'This,' he continued, 'is a diagram of what is known as the Elizabeth Buckholz murder, which occurred in a cemetery, on 13 September 1908, a few miles out of Berlin, at a point sparsely populated.

'The body was found twenty-four hours after the crime. Frack and his trainer, summoned from Berlin, were put on the case. This red line which you see starting from the cemetery and meandering about the chart shows the route taken by Frack after starting from the scene of the murder and continues to the spot where he found the evidence through which the guilty man was afterward located in Berlin.

'The distance covered by the dog was about three kilometres, two miles, let us say. From the clothing of Elizabeth Buckholz, Frack got the first scent, which he lost for a few hundred yards and again picked up at this point marked with a red "X". Again he lost it. We come down along this roadway, across a field, through another open road, across the railroad track into a station that during the intervening twenty-four hours had been occupied by not less than two hundred people; a difficult territory for a dog depending upon his nose.

'But Frack here picked up the spoor, followed it through the station and down to the highway, where he was again baffled but in no sense defeated. Observe now how he began to range about the neighbourhood in an uncertain, groping endeavour.

'He takes to a stubble field and covers it like a bird dog. Ah, he has it. Here another "X" the end of the trail.

In the autumn-dried grass lies a bicycle discarded by the murderer, after he had ridden three kilometres from the scene of his crime. In that distance he had dismounted thrice, once a few hundred yards from the cemetery, once in the depot station, and here at the point of leaving the machine.

'Frack, at this juncture, seemed to realize that he had completed his work in running down the bicycle. He walked around it several times, sniffed at the handle bars and there upon, although still in leash to his trainer, proceeded with his nose, teeth and paws to push and pull back into the road, where it belonged, this thing he had brought forth as evidence.

'Now, my dear sir, up to this point Frack had followed his instincts and trusted to his nose, which is all that a police dog is expected to do. But he went a step farther and exercised what seemed to have been reason.

'He seemed to say in dog language: "There it is. I've done my part. Now do yours." The bicycle proved to be the property of one Waldenburg, who had murdered the woman in a fit of jealousy. He went to his death cursing Frack, who survived his victim many years, and, as the best dog detective in the service, added new laurels to his fame.

'Whether or not he possessed reasoning power is for you to decide. We think he did. In any event, this branch of the service agrees with whoever supplied the motto for the police dog department.'

George Gazlow pointed to a German text quotation on the wall: 'The more I see of men, the more I admire dogs.'

Robert Davies, *The More I Admire Dogs*, 1936

Grave Matters

THE DOG OF which I speak was a terrier. It showed its affection in the most marked manner in several ways. Every morning, as soon as it got out of the kitchen, it came to its master's door, and if not admitted and caressed about the usual hour, gave evident signs of impatience.

It would lie quiet till it thought the time had arrived, but never longer. Afterwards it went to the breakfast-room, and occupied its master's chair till he arrived. On one occasion a visitor was in the house, who, coming first into the room, ordered the dog to come off the best chair. To this it paid no attention, and when threatened with expulsion, at once prepared for defence. But as soon as its master appeared it resigned its place voluntarily, and quietly stretched itself on the rug at his feet.

At another time it was left for three weeks during its master's absence from home. It saw him leave in a steamer, and every day until his return it repaired to the quay upon the arrival of the same boat, expecting him to come again in the one by which he had gone.

It distinguished between a number of boats, always selecting the right one and the right hour. One evening it accompanied its master when he went to gather mussels for bait. As the tide was far in, few mussels remained uncovered; and after collecting all within reach, more were required. A large bunch lay a few feet from the water's edge, but beyond reach; yet as the dog was not one of those who take to the water to fetch, its master had no expectation that it would prove useful on the present occasion.

Seeing him looking at the mussels, however, it first took a good look at those in the basket, and then, without being directed at all, went into the water. Selecting the right bunch from among the stones and wreck with which it was surrounded, it brought it to land, and laid it at its master's feet. This, I think, is a proof of reasoning, rather than of instinct. The dog had never been trained to go into the sea, and would not probably have brought out the mussels had it not seen that they were wanted.

It showed wonderful instinct, however, just before the death of one of its pups, and before its own death. Its pup had not been thriving, and the mother gave unmistakable proof that she foresaw its death.

She dug a grave for it and put it in. Nor, when it was removed, would she let it lie beside her, but immediately dug another grave, where she was less likely to be disturbed. On the day of her own death, also, she used what strength she had to dig her own grave and she insisted on lying in it until her eyes glazed over and she was no more.

The Spectator, 10 June 1876

Chapter Six

MAD OWNERS

Nipper

Nipper was a mongrel of very mixed ancestry. She had hints of Irish wolfhound and a touch of lurcher, yet somehow she managed also to suggest to the casual observer that a poodle had left its mark somewhere in the distant past.

Nipper – an absurd name one might say for such a large and robust dog – was one of those animals that charms everyone. Visitors to the house found Nipper paying close attention to them the instant they stepped through the front door. She didn't bark or overly pester but she would behave as if each and every visitor was the centre and wellspring of her life.

Dr Widdup, who had owned Nipper from puppyhood, was at first a little jealous that Nipper should behave toward comparative strangers as she might have been expected to behave towards him – he, after all, provided her with bed and board, endless delightful treats, exciting walks through rabbit filled meadows, visits to doting relatives and everything else a dog could possibly require. Yet the habit of devotion to strangers persisted.

Dr Widdup may have felt aggrieved that Nipper was not as good to him as he was to strangers but the general delight felt by his friends at the attentions they received from a dog agreed to be a paragon was some compensation.

Then Nipper suddenly changed tack. She began to be indifferent to visitors and developed a more eccentric habit. Two, three or even more times each week she would return from the fields with a live rabbit, a hedgehog or even on one occasion a pigeon clamped firmly but gently in her jaws. As soon as she dropped these offerings at her master's feet they would scurry or fly away. Usually they were dropped near enough to the open door to make their escape without difficulty, but occasionally Dr Widdup would be forced to spend a great deal of time removing a rabbit from under a sideboard, a chair or a longcase clock.

Things reached a crisis when Nipper brought home a large rat which, when released, hid behind a massive oak dresser. Dr Widdup had no intention of dismantling such a large piece of furniture and he knew anyway that the rat would simply run for cover to another piece of furniture long before anything practical could be done to remove it form the house.

His solution was to borrow a high powered air rifle from a neighbour and lie on the floor taking pot shots at the rat which had an uncanny ability to jump six inches along the skirting board just before the good doctor managed to fire each shot. Eventually a pellet struck home and the problem was solved.

But ever after Dr Widdup kept the door of the house firm closed while Nipper was enjoying a run outside. As soon as she barked to be let in she was forced to release whichever animal she had decided to bring to the house on that particular day. Dr Widdup imagined that these gifts were perhaps Nipper's way of making up for that long period during which she made more of strangers than she made of the good doctor.

John O'London's, January 1922

Topsy Turvy

I HAD A DOG called Topsy for ten years and in that time I made no attempt to teach her anything.

She had a delightful habit when I returned home in the evening of leaping four feet into the air and always with the expectation that I would catch her. I always did.

When the Hansom cab dropped me at the door it was my habit to throw off my boots in the hall and find out my soft felt shoes. One day Topsy leaped into my arms, licked my face, jumped down, ran off and returned with first one felt shoe then the other. I was both astonished and not a little delighted.

What would she do next? I soon found the answer.

She saw me pull the curtains in my bedroom when it was time to retire and before she was a year old she would attempt to do it for me. The curtains, on an old rail, did not run smoothly so I had the rail polished and she pulled both curtains across at night and back again in the morning from then on.

I reached a point where I dare not let her out of my sight imagining that her astonishing qualities would be clear to all we passed in the street and that she would be stolen.

I took to carrying her everywhere in a large inside pocket I had specially sewn into my coat. There she would curl up silently whether I walked across the city or took myself into a Hansom cab.

I guarded her jealously and raged against God when she died. She had shared my meals, slept at the end of my bed and waited often for hours outside the British Museum, the chop house and the Athenaeum without complaint. I had not the heart to get another dog after she had gone.

John Masters, *In Spite of All*, 1880

Soloist

WHEN SOMEONE plays an instrument, dogs howl. I have
been told this is due to the fact that some dogs have more
sensitive ears than others, that music is so piercing it pains
them, and their singing or howling isn't an expression of
pleasure but of discomfort.

I don't accept that explanation, though, because dogs
are sometimes attracted by music. I have seen them sit
and sing without making any effort to escape. When A.
Ducasse was a boy, he took lessons on the French horn.
His father owned four young coon hounds, brothers, that
lived in the barn. But when young A. would start practis-
ing on his horn, the hounds would come up to the house,
sit in a semicircle under his window and howl as he tooted.

They were such good harmonizers that his mother
named them Soprano, Alto, Tenor and Bass.

The best soloist I ever heard was a little Boston Terrier,
Pat, owned by O. R. Rickel. Mr Rickel actually trained this
Mutt to the point that whenever he pulled out his har-
monica and started blowing it, Pat always joined in. He
usually warmed up in the lower registers, looking straight
ahead and rolling his popeyes.

Eventually it took just a hand signal from his owner
to get him to howl any one of six different tunes – and
Rickel could by raising a certain number of fingers choose
the tune.

That little dog became the talk of the state and earned a packet for his owners. One man offered a thousand dollars to buy him, but Rickel wouldn't have taken ten thousand dollars for that dog.

Eldon Roarke, *Just a Mutt*, 1947

Dash It!

CHARLES ROBERT LESLIE, the painter, relates that Queen Victoria was always very fond of dogs, and one very singular circumstance occurred on the day of her coronation in 1837.

Her Majesty had one favourite little spaniel, who was always on the lookout for her return when she had been from home. She had of course been separated from him on that day longer than usual, and when the state coach drove up to the steps of the palace, she heard him barking with joy in the hall, and exclaimed, 'There's Dash,' and threw aside the sceptre and orb she carried in her hands, took off the crown and robes and insisted that she must go off at once to wash Dash.

Charles Williams, *Anecdotes of Dogs*, 1870

Urine Sample

Charles II that goodly king had a favourite dog, among several that he did love, a spaniel that greatly did amuse him, more even he confessed than did my Lord of Rochester. Rochester, that merry dog, got up a great heap of vile poems that did much affect the king. The dog got up against the king's leg and did piss on him.

Barnaby Green, A True Word or None, 1790

Revolutionary Dog

An English gentleman, incarcerated in a French prison and under sentence of death during the French Revolution came into possession of a little dog to which he became very strongly attached.

An offer of escape was made him for consideration, when he was told the dog must be left behind; but this he declared could not be, and assured his jailer that the animal would fully attend to any orders he gave it.

After a time the jailor agreed to the experiment. A large hamper was brought into the cell one evening; the gentleman now addressed the dog very earnestly, especially telling it that it must not make any noise he then, with the dog, laid himself down in the hamper, which was carefully packed and sent to the nearest sea port during the night.

All the next day the hamper lay about the wharf as if it were of no value, but at night it was, as previously arranged, carefully taken on board a vessel, and a few hours after the gentleman was once more safe on English ground; the dog, from first to last, not having uttered a single sound. The faithful animal was now more highly prized than ever, and a place was assigned it regularly at the table of its master.

Had he been caught both dog and man would have lost their lives but as he said often in the coming years life without his dog would not have been worth the candle.

Charles Williams, *Anecdotes of Dogs*, 1870

Whippet Supreme

WHIPPET RACING has long been in vogue among the coal miners. It was they who brought the breed to its present high state of perfection. Not until recently has it come to be regarded as a top sport for the élite. Its sudden popularity dates from the time when several years ago a promoter with a wise head brought down to Hurlingham, just outside London, a carefully selected string of whippets – with their coal-dusted owners.

It was a new sensation to the sporting gentry of England. The leaping shadows in pursuit of the mechanical hare, the rapidity of the betting, the antics of the men from Armadale, the thrill of the straining finish, did the trick.

Whippet racing took London by storm. The coal miners went mad sympathetically. The noble thoroughbred was pitted in a speed contest against the coal miner's dog.

Muntaz Mahal, a racehorse, did a specified distance at the rate of thirty-nine miles an hour against the whippet's thirty-six. The dog came into his own. Courses were erected everywhere and whippets went up in price. They jumped from five pounds to ten, twenty, thirty – a hundred. One sold in London for four thousand pounds.

Parks, stadiums, racetracks and open lots, long idle, were drafted for the whippets. Capitalists crawled out from under their hoards and supplied the sinews for development.

I spent a most exciting evening at an Armadale straight away track, where many of the fastest dogs in Scotland get their training. Whippet men from this region are per sons of parts and speaketh by the card. They be oracles, and no man may gainsay them.

Armadale owners, at the signal to 'go', pitch their whippets down the course by the scruff of the neck and a tail hold. The dogs hit the turf at thirty miles an hour without missing stride. The goal is a fluttering kerchief. Everybody backs a favourite and much change circulates.

Occasionally a bookmaker welshes and fans are treated to the spectacle of a desperate man breaking all records across the moor.

From an Armadale schoolteacher on my right I picked up a good story about a miner who owned Annie Laurie, a fast whippet that he had been training on selected beef-steak.

'Meat,' said the pedagogue, 'that should have gone to the man's family.' The wife was ill but made no complaint. Shortly before the race the woman came to a point where rich meat broth was necessary to sustain her vitality. The miner saw the handwriting on the wall. He felt that the winning of the race would replenish his funds, but he couldn't feed the woman and the whippet beef-steak at the same time.

He took counsel with his son, a boy of twelve, and agreed that if the worst came to the worst the woman should have the meat and the whippet would be withdrawn at the last moment.

'But, laddie,' said the father, 'I canna bring mesel' to tak the meat fra' the whuppet. Ye will ha' to do that.'

The boy took the precious morsel to his mother. What did the woman do but decline it. The father, torn between love of the dog and duty to the woman for the moment disappeared.

By command of his heroic mother the son fed the whippet the last piece of meat and groomed the hope of the family for the supreme test. When the race was called the youngster himself pitched the animal down the course and saw the finish, with his entry two lengths in the lead.

Steak for the whole family! That whippet sold the next day for two hundred and ten pounds – a high price indeed. From the strain of the race Annie never recovered and the buyer, convinced finally that he had purchased a dog that had all but broken its heart in a last effort, returned the animal to the Armadale miner with the comment 'Annie Laurie is a house dog, and belongs at home wi' the wee children'.

Robert Davies, *The More I Admire Dogs*, 1936

Preaching Companion

A WEST COUNTRY vicar became so devoted to his spaniel that he refused to preach if the dog was not in attendance. His parishioners were delighted as the dog's antics brightened an otherwise dull service for the clergyman was famous for his dull sermons.

At first the dog would simply sit quietly at the foot of the steps leading up to the pulpit, occasionally wandering off to investigate an odd little movement in a dark corner of the church or greeting a special friend in the congregation.

But news of the dog's presence reached the bishop

when the vicar began to throw titbits to his dog at intervals during each and every service. After a while the dog learned to expect these treats and if they were not forthcoming he would bark. To mollify him the vicar threw more titbits down until the air seemed filled with flying scraps of bacon and cheese and mutton.

The congregation increased significantly as word spread through the villages of these Sunday events but inevitably the bishop became concerned at what was going on and visited the church to see for himself.

He was so outraged that he interrupted the service and denounced the parson who calmly left the pulpit and then the church. A week later the ecclesiastical courts began a process that would lead to the loss of his living. Rumour insisted that the vicar had refused even to consider getting rid of his dog. No doubt this is the first – and perhaps only – instance of a dog being chosen in preference to a call to the ministry.

Western Morning News, August 1869

Pooch or Infant

FOR THE FIRST twenty years of their existence the railway companies charged very high fares for pets. The feeling was that animals were a bit of a nuisance and might
put off other passengers. High prices would ensure that
only the absolutely determined would take Rover or Tid-
dles with them. And if they could afford the high prices
the pet owners were far more likely to turn up with a
spotless poodle rather than a muddy hound, thus reduc
ing the risk of complaints from other passengers.

The high price policy seemed to be having the desired
effect, but then rumours began to circulate that passengers were avoiding paying for the pets in the most in-
genious way.

An official employed by one company to find out what
was going on reported one incident to the board: 'I was
aboard the down train for Nottingham keeping my wits
about me and observing the very mixed crowd in the
second class carriages. We stopped at a country station
and a woman got into the carriage carrying a ponderous
looking babe. It was dressed in long clothes and with its
head entirely concealed in a shawl.

'Several times during the journey the half smothered
infant made a noise very like the barking of a dog. The
repetition of these unusual sounds aroused the sympathy
of another passenger, an old lady, who remarked: "What

a dreadful cold that child has got to be sure." The woman with the baby replied that the poor thing had suffered an attack of the flu which she was afraid would turn to whooping cough.

'At Nottingham the ticket collector opened the door abruptly and shouted "Tickets please!" the suddenness of this outburst clearly surprised the slumbering object in the woman's arms and there was an angry and un-mistakable bark. The astonished ticket collector reached forward and before the woman could object he lifted the shawl to reveal a not particularly attractive nor youthful Dachshund.'

The official report does not say what happened next but it is easy to imagine that the poor woman would have had to pay the extra fare amid hoots of laughter from the other passengers.

The Observer, 1885

Going to Church

THE ROYAL FAMILY, while at Balmoral, are accustomed to attend Crathie Church, where some instances of canine sagacity were, and may still be, observable.

A fine large dog, if I remember rightly, of the New-foundland race, was accustomed gravely to follow the clergyman to his pulpit, and on his closing the door, to take up his position on the top stair, where he remained – a very model of propriety – to the close of the service.

The Queen and Prince Albert became, very naturally, interested in so intelligent an animal, and when it was absent from its place in church on one occasion, they made kindly inquiry respecting it. The Queen observed wryly that the service was much improved by the presence of the dog.

One Sunday morning the clergyman left home, attended by his dog, and after proceeding some distance, met his ministerial brother, with whom it was arranged he should make an exchange of services; and after some salutations of mutual friendliness, he went on his way. But now a question arose evidently in the dog's mind as to the course he should take – either to accompany his master to the neighbouring church, or return with the visitor to his own.

Having 'set his canine brains to comprehend the case', he decided on the latter, followed the clergyman for the day up the pulpit stairs, and laid himself down in his accustomed place.

In pastoral parts of Scotland, it is usual for each shepherd to take his faithful collie into the church; and in a district of Sutherland, where the population is very scanty, congregations may be said to consist of two portions; the one half shepherds, and the other half dogs.

Like their masters these dogs enjoy the Gaelic sermons
and services far more than the English; but sometimes, as
might be expected, an amusing circumstance occurs.

A clergyman, being annoyed during his sermon by the
restlessness and occasional whining of a dog, which at last
began to bark outright, looked about, as the dog's master
was absent, for the beadle, and said, very peremptorily,
'John, carry that dog out.'

John looked up instantly to the pulpit, and with anything but a face expressing obedience, said, 'Na, na, sir; I'll
just mak him gae oot on his ain foor legs.'

On another occasion, a dog was present during the
service, where the worthy minister, getting warm in
his sermon, was in the habit of speaking very loud, and
even shouting almost to the top of his voice. The dog,
who in the early part of the service had been very quiet,
became now greatly excited, as is not uncommon with
some dogs when hearing a noise, and after 'whining as
the clergyman's voice rose, at last began to bark and howl
– a tumult which, probably, would have been stopped at
the outset had its master been present. The clergyman,
naturally annoyed at the interruption, directed the beadle
to put out the dog, who, unlike the one just described, at
once expressed his readiness to obey the order, but could
not resist the temptation to look up to the pulpit and say,
very significantly, "Ay, ay, sir, but indeed it was yersell
began it."'

When many dogs are present at church, it is not unusual for them all to be still till towards the end of the last Psalm, when there is a general stretching and yawning, and they are all ready to scamper out, barking in the greatest excitement, whenever the benediction is commenced. The congregation of one of these churches determined, therefore, that the services should close in a decorous manner, and steps were taken to secure this being done. Accordingly, when a stranger was officiating, he was surprised to find all the people sitting down when he was about to pronounce the blessing, and consequently paused, expecting them to rise. An old shepherd, who observed his hesitation, ended it by looking up to the pulpit with the charge: 'Say awa', sir, we're a' sitting to cheat the dawgs.'

I knew a dog well who never went, as some others do, to church or chapel; but while his master and mistress were there, he occupied himself in a very peculiar way. As soon as they were gone, he mounted a chest of drawers or a dressing-table at the bedroom window, and when I have been returning from Divine Service, I have often seen him – a beautiful specimen of his race – looking out for their return; and directly he caught sight of them, he quitted his lookout, bounded down the stairs and danced a jig on his back two legs as they came through the door.

R. P. S. Trinder, *A Way to the Hills*, 1899

Legacy

SAMUEL WILLIAMS inherited a great deal of money on the death of his father in 1730. Thereafter he decided that his proper course was to live the life of a gentleman which meant doing as little as possible beyond eating, drinking and visiting the playhouse.

By the age of thirty Samuel had grown immensely stout and gouty. He was a member of several London clubs and would breakfast in one, take lunch in the next and have dinner in a third. His routine almost never varied. He refused to walk anywhere and made his coachman wait outside each of his clubs in all weathers.

He never married but in his fortieth year, on the recommendation of a friend, he bought two greyhounds. Within weeks he ceased to visit his clubs and his friends and acquaintances saw nothing of him.

At home he dined with his new companions – the greyhounds – had beds made up for them in his own room and employed a young man to take them regularly to the park.

The young man was given strict instructions to say nothing to anyone of his master's habits or whereabouts. In short Williams became a recluse and a miserly one at that.

When some five years later he died it was revealed that he had left all his money – several thousand pounds and two properties – to the two greyhounds with strict instructions as to how they should be treated, how they should be fed, housed and exercised.

In his will he apologised for so far indulging his pets and promised that on the death of the dogs his entire estate should go to Coram's Fields, the foundling hospital. But he appointed also an executor to ensure that his wishes were carried out. If the dogs were neglected he said Coram would get nothing.

The Spectator, June 1770

Lost and Found

A CLERK WHO came on duty at the Parcel Office of a Manchester station, had not been long at the counter when a furious passenger appeared and asked whether a dog that he had previously brought to the office, to be sent to the Liverpool Dog Show, had been despatched to Liverpool by the 11.15 am train as had specifically been requested.

The clerk looked over the entries in his log book, and finding the dog duly entered for the train named, told the passenger it had been sent. In response the passenger shouted at the top of his voice: 'It's a damned lie!' Somewhat nettled at this outburst, the clerk explained he could produce the porter who had put the dog into the train, so he was startled by the passenger saying: 'Young man, can you explain how it is that when I got home I found that very same dog you claim to have sent to Liverpool sitting on my door step here in Manchester?'

This appeared so impossible that the clerk immediately dashed off to get the porter who was responsible for putting the dog into the train, and on finding him on the platform, bellowed:

'Charlie, did you take a dog for the Liverpool Show to the 11.15 am?'

'Yes, I did; what about it?'

'Well, there's a gentleman in the office who says that when he got home he found the dog sitting on his doorstep.'

'Did he, now? We'll, I'm not surprised.'

'But how could that be if you sent it off by the 11.15?'

'Well, you know, it was like this. When the man brought the dog to the office, it was in a hamper, and he had so much to say about it that Cook (another porter) and I thought we'd like to look at it. So we opened the hamper, and no sooner had we got the lid up than the little beggar jumped out, and bolted through the door, with Cook and I after it as hard as we could go. We followed it down Hunts Bank and along into Deansgate, where it turned off and went over the bridge into Salford, where, although we did our best to overtake it, we lost sight of it altogether. We looked at each other in dismay, and then, a happy thought occurring to me, I said to Cook, "I'm not going back without a dog. I'll have the first dog I see," so I got a dog and brought it back with me to the station, and that dog's gone to Liverpool.'

Charlie agreed to see the sender of the dog, and make a clean breast of it. Fortunately the humour of the situation appeared to strike the gentleman who, after administering a good-humoured rebuke to the porter, said he would bring the dog back, on a chain, for a later train, and that there was to be no mistake about sending it forward this time.

The sequel to the story is that on the following day a hamper containing a dejected looking dog of uncertain breed was returned to Manchester from Liverpool, with the following endorsement on the label: 'The Secretary of the Liverpool Dog Show declines to exhibit the animal contained herein – cannot classify!'

Land and Water, June 1959

Royal Warning

THE PRINCESS VICTORIA, when twelve years old, and on a visit at Bushey Park, in Middlesex, was cautioned against a dog she was disposed to caress, as one whose temper was so uncertain as to render any reliance on it undesirable; but she still thought it was so well disposed to herself as to show it some kindness.

Growler at length proved that his character had not
been maligned, by making a snap at her hand, which was
stretched out to him as usual: her Royal Highness's attendant expressed much concern at this, when the Princess
replied, 'Oh, thank you; you are right and I was wrong,
but see how intelligent he is; he chose only to warn me a
little and not to bite. I will be more careful how I address
him in future.'

The Times, August 1825

Hunting First, War Second

Nothing illustrates the English obsession with hunting better than a story from the Napoleonic wars. The
English under Wellington were encamped in a highly
dangerous position and had been under fire for some
time when a lull in hostilities gave both French and British
soldiers a chance to recuperate.

It is a bizarre fact of history that when campaigning,
Wellington always took his foxhounds with him – when
there was time he could indulge his favourite pastime.

During a lull in the fighting the hounds were enjoying
an outing when a fox got up and was chased close to the
French lines. The hunt master shouted that the chase should
be called off but a young officer who perhaps should have
known better would have none of it and shouted: 'Where

the hounds go I follow' and regardless of the danger of being shot or captured he set off in full cry.

Needless to say the hounds crossed into enemy territory and the young officer was captured by the French.

The French, who knew nothing of fox hunting, were baffled. What was this young English officer doing with a large number of scruffy looking dogs on their side of the line? The young man's explanation was so astonishing that they believed him and he was returned – along with his hounds – unharmed to the British lines.

Shooting Times, 16 July 1928

No Human Friends

A GENTLEMAN living in Southwark had the reputation for being immensely wealthy. He was also known to be exceedingly fond of dogs. Indeed his fondness for dogs far exceeded any fellow feeling he might have for his fellow man.

He lived at the end of an unprepossessing and very narrow street that turned off west from the main thoroughfare after you cross London Bridge and enter the Borough.

The street and the houses it once contained are long gone, but a few older people still remember Powell the dog man.

He dressed in the fashion of an earlier age, still wearing a powdered wig long after such things had gone out of fashion. He wore knee breeches and a velvet coat and was always accompanied by two or three dogs. But the odd thing about the dogs, which stuck very close by him despite being entirely unleashed, was that he had a different dog, or dogs, for different days of the week.

Two spaniels and a mongrel accompanied him to lunch on Mondays; a mastiff and her daughter on Tuesday; a bulldog, of the kind favoured by the painter Hogarth, was his sole companion on Wednesday, and two pointers on Thursday. On Friday the mongrel, clearly a favourite, might re-appear or some other combination of all the other dogs. It was said that Powell had formerly taken all the dogs to lunch with him each day but that other diners had objected to the noise of their yelping and snuffling and barking. They also sat and lay all about old Powell's table while he dined and other diners tripped over the recumbent hounds.

In ones and twos and threes the dogs were tolerable, indeed well behaved and would instantly do their master's bidding whatever that might be. He always ordered three chops and a deal of ham but ate little himself. The food was distributed among the dogs. What was particularly noticeable was that each dog took its morsel from the old man's hand with the utmost gentleness and grace. Here was no desperate rushing and snapping, no intemperate rush to snap up the trifles offered to them.

The mongrel was permitted to sit upon its master's lap and often, as a result, enjoyed the more delicate morsels.

At the end of his dinner Powell would rise, throw down some coins and leave without a word. The dining house was but a few dozen yards from his house, but Powell never walked further afield, nor were the dogs ever seen abroad at any other time than dinner.

Powell in short was a man of some mysteriousness. One man only claimed to have seen the inside of his house. Rumour everywhere said that Powell was rich and that the house, tall, narrow and very old, was filled with gold, but no burglar would attempt to enter for the dogs that seemed so mild in the street and the dining house had the reputation of savagery at home. It was said among the riverside gangs that one of their number had been almost eaten alive after entering Powell's house at night.

When the old man finally died the dogs at the funeral outnumbered greatly those human friends and relatives who walked the last mile to his grave.

The London Journal, March 1850

BARKING MAD

Beggars Belief

A LONDON beggar had a most remarkable dog which he had trained to do all manner of tricks to excite the sympathy of the populace and to entertain them.

The beggar came every week to his patch opposite my mother's house in Grove Park, Camberwell. These were the houses of the better off and the beggar clearly thought that here any pennies dropped into his hat might be transmuted into shillings or gold sovereigns.

The beggar wore a padded coat tied with string and had a full beard that made him seem not unlike His Majesty Edward VII. His coat had many pockets and when a few children had gathered round him he would stare about theatrically and begin to search first this pocket then that.

At last he would pull out a long wooden flute. He would shout, 'Behold' while holding flute and arms aloft. Then he would begin to play a jolly tune and he was a very talented player.

Immediately his little terrier – which had sat patiently to one side during these preliminaries – would jump to its feet and move to a position exactly in front of the beggar and facing the little audience. It would then begin to turn backward and forward somersaults in the most extraordinary fashion while running in a circle in between jumps.

After a minute or two the beggar would stop, look about him and make a show of packing his things to move on. The children knew if they wanted more entertainment they would need to drop a penny or two in the hat he had carefully left till last.

He would peer into the hat and if a penny or two could be seen he would begin the next part of his little act which involved the little dog dancing on its back legs and twirling about.

The children, though they had seen this and the dog's other tricks before, would clap their hands in delight. By this time one or two adults would be on their doorsteps along with kitchen maids and errand boys peering from the area railings.

The finale would come at last and the little dog, to the accompaniment of a drum roll played with a flourish by the beggar, would push a series of cunningly contrived levers on the beggar's brightly painted handcart. Each lever released a different delight – a jack in the box from here, a balloon from there and, finally, a white dove that flew away over the high trees.

The beggar would then nod and smile and tidy his things away before setting off down the hill with the little terrier happily running behind.

The London Gazette, 1864

BIBLIOGRAPHY

Newspapers and Magazines

Bristol Mercury

British Chronicle

Country Times

Gamekeeper, The

Gentleman's magazine, The

Glasgow Herald

Illustrated London News

John O'London's

Land and Water

London Gazette, The

London Journal, The

Morning Chronicle, The

National Review

Newcastle Chronicle

Observer, The

Railway Times

Shooting Times and Country magazine

Spectator, The

Sportsman, The

The Times

Western Morning News

Books

Art and Sport, 1936

Baker, Peter Shaw, *Dog Heroes*, 1935

Brown, Ivor, *London Memories*, 1947

Coventry, Francis, *The History of Pompey the Little*, 1751

Davies, Robert, *The More I Admire Dogs*, 1936

Eccentric Lives, Keogh Press, 1955

Edwards, E.W., *Thoughts on Fishing*, 1926

Fahey, A. *Isis and Oxon*, 1906

Fletcher, Lionel, *Skipper My Chum*, 1935

Gask, L., *Not Worth His Salt*, 1910

Giles, Martin, *Railway Memories* (unpublished memoir)

Green, Barnaby, *True Word or None*, 1790

Jackman, Francis, *Journeyman*, 1867

Jensen, Peter, *High Days and Holidays*, 1922

L'Histoire des Chiens Celebres, Paris, 1818

Masters, John, *In Spite of All*, 1880

Matlock, A.J.T, *River of Dreams*, 1938

Our Dumb Animals, 1930

Pepys, Samuel, *Diary*, Penguin, 2003

Quinn, Tom, *Fish Tales*, Alan Sutton, 1992

Quinn, Tom, *Shooting's Strangest Days*, Robson Books, 2002

Quinn, Tom, *Tales from the Water's Edge*, David & Charles, 1992

Roarke, Eldon, *Just a Mutt*, 1947

Seeley, E. O, and Lane M.A.L., *Chinook and His Family*, 1930

Smith, J. B. H., *Memories*, 1913

Trinder, R. P. S., *A Way to the Hills*, 1899

Wadham, C., *The Cart Before the Horse*

Ward, Robin, *Mad Science*, 1950

Williams, Charles, *Anecdotes of Dogs*, 1870

Williams, R. S. V., *Sport for All*, 1909

Every reasonable effort has been made by the editor to trace copyright holders of material reproduced in this book, but if any have been inadvertently overlooked the publishers would be glad to hear from them.